Still Mind, Singing Heart

Poetry of the Spirit

These lines are sunbeams from the soul, like the ring of fire, in a total eclipse. For some, these can serve as bridges between Knowledge and Understanding

ISBN 979-8-89186-937-0

From the Spirit, to the Spirit

What some readers say:

"A celebration of life, death and everything in between, this collection is a mystical tribute to the soul and the human condition."

- Kiran Manral

"These poems ignite a yearning for something primordial."

– Unmesh Dewan

"Persevere in trying to get to the root of what K is saying. This may lead you to a spiritual flowering and - dare I say this? - ecstasy!"

– Prof. Srikumar Rao

"K's poems know no barriers where it comes to faith, culture, or any other such divide. He appears to soar far above all such trivialities".

– Iqbal Khamis

"A very simple guide lamp for all who search for their own souls."

– Lt. Col. Ankush Goyal

"K's ability to describe in poems what I feel, but can't express, is uncanny."

– Shobha Mathur

It is such a pleasure to read your thoughts.
Very enriching.

– Brig (retd) Sanjay Agarwal

These writing successfully evoke a connection
between the divine and personal emotions.
I have to re-read them several times - each time
I learn from them!

– Rashmi Mishra

These poems are mystical, deep and expression
of a sensitive, inquisitive and searching mind.
They will delight many, haunt many and resonate
with many of the readers.

– Brij Chopra

STILL MIND, SINGING HEART

Index at the end

My Poems

When the mind is still,
And no sounds intrude,
Soft words emerge, seemingly apart,
And become poems in my heart.

It may just be an illusion,
But, then, what is not?

ભ્ઙ્ભ્ઙ્ભ્ઙ

Becoming

Some time back,
My heart reached out,
And touched my mind.
In this happy marriage,
I was re-born.

My words are an expression,
An announcement, if you will,
Of my becoming.

ઙ

A Weaver I Am

I weave my baskets with reeds of words,
And fill them with flowers from my heart,
Grown lovingly by my liminal self,
Tinted by colours from every part.

Some are pink with feelings soft,
Some are red with passion true.
Some are purple with my laughter,
Some are sadly very blue.

And you'll find, in these pages,
White ones, pure, sublime,
Compassion's gentle smile,
That turns mere prose to rhyme.

So I weave, now and then
And whenever I have one new,
A basket full of who I am,
I offer it, humbly to you.

The Password

When you reach the Beloved's door,
And you want to enter,
Don't knock or call,
For I have been told,
The password is soundless.

ଔଷଔଷଔଷ

Come join us......

We are a tribe of more than a few,
Who live in the old, as well as the new.
The Dark is our friend, and Light our mate.
Life writes on both sides of our slate.

We leave none untouched with who we are,
In many planes, near and far.

We dance with the fairies and walk with the ghosts.
We sing the sweetest, we love the most.

If all knew, we are but them;
Flowers, leaves, roots & stem.

Yes,

We are the valley, we are the hill,
Make of us, what you will.
Join us and you'll understand.
You've always been of our merry band.
Give up your mind, open your heart.
Be one with the world, that would be a start.

We never grow old, we never tire,
The fire never goes out in our fire.

We wait for you, as we've always done,
And will keep waiting for every one.

Come………

ଔଓଔଓଔଓ

The Wave

My mind flits from desire to desire,
Craving ice now, and then fire,
Forming the wave I call my life

Till one day, it meets the sea.
All is calm, there's no Me.
No "who" nor "what" nor "why".
No "am", just I.

ଔଔଔ

I AM....

Complete in my Self, fully free,
I am all that I can be.
I am That all the time.
I am its prose, I am its rhyme.

Not for me pilgrimages galore,
Or visits to seers, door to door.
Wherever I look, there I am.
My holy land is where I am.

Qamar - The Moon

There are those,
Who spend their lives arguing,
Which is better,
The crescent moon
Or the full.

Then there are a few,
Who revel in both,
For they know,
The Moon is One!

ଓଃଙ୍ଗଓଃଙ୍ଗଓଃଙ୍ଗ

On the wayside...

I saw a signboard,
On the Path to becoming Whole:
The Soul isn't in 'you';

'*You' are in the Soul*!

ଓଃଡ଼ଓଃଡ଼ଓଃଡ଼

On Becoming

I walk through Becoming,
A long veranda at sunset,
Pillars of shadow,
Squares of sunshine,
Life and death,
Which is which,
I know no more.

One-ness

In deep sleep,
I shall peep at my Self,
And thine,
Both equally divine
And newly born in the morn,
I'll be the knower and the known;
The painter and the sign.

ଓଃଓଃଓଃ

Names of God

Three thousand names of God,
Three hundred or three.
They do not do as much to me,
As one good deed done, unknown.
One seed unselfishly sown.

Ana al Haq – I am the Truth

I whirled around,
Hopeful, unsure,
Till I saw the Divine,
And danced no more.

Strange as it may sound,
I paused, looked around,
And burst out laughing!

ઉ૪ઉ૪ઉ૪

At Heaven's Door

I visited God last night,
Or his closed door, to be precise.
On it was written, in letters bold,
Entry barred, to Mind or Gold.

Alas, my mind was with me,
On its high horse,
Full of knowledge,
Richly adorned,
And I had to turn back unfulfilled.

But my heart,
Caught a glimpse of the Beloved
And on the way back it whispered……
"There was no door."

Looking for 'my' Self…

I reach out for Jesus,
And he smiles at me from the mirror.
I search for Rama,
And find him serene in my heart.
When I call Krishna,
Who I hold so dear,
My echo is all I hear.

And so it goes,
As from door to door,
I seek Buddhas galore,
Looking for my Self

ઉ૪ઉ૪ઉ૪

A longing...

Beloved,
Let me whirl in your heart, tonight,
As you have done so long in mine.

Keep your door ajar,
For though I know
What you're like, inside me,
I am dying to see,
If I am the same inside you!

ଔଔଔ

Finally,

All desires melt,
And in melting,
Are no more.

The body goes, then
And the mind, sensing it not,
Is lost in unaccustomed solitude,
And it soon blinks out.

Lamenter and lament,
Gone unlamented without logic,
Beyond sense and sensibility.

Bells and trumpets fade,
And I shine in all my glory,
As I always was,
As you always are.

Harmony

Soft bells in the dark, like a mystic chime,
Take my heartbeats, and make them rhyme,
With the cosmic hum, pure, sublime,
Till I become one, with eternal time.

Made of wool of many a kind,
In this rough rug, I suddenly find,
A shahtoosh shawl, smooth and fine,
Glowing golden, in the light divine.

ଔଔଔ

To Each His World, His Unique God

This life and time, this grief and sorrow,
This give and take, this lend and borrow,
To love and hate, be kind and unkind,
Is it all done with mirrors of the mind?

Roots

I want to go back,
To the cumulative intellect,
That spawned me,
So that I may know,
Who they were,
And who I am.

It is not enough to say 'Om'.
One must know,
What came before Amen.

ଔଓଔଓଔଓ

The Here & Now

Passions stilled,
Emotionless, without desire,
I sit in the centre of incandescence,
And life beckons,
For time is not now.
I leave reluctantly,
One womb
For another,
Which I had left,
As unwillingly
                    before.

I Would Like

I would like my mind to know how,
Not to think just clever thoughts,
But to dwell in cosmic silence,
In the midst of noises loud.

I would like my senses to feel now,
Not pleasures, just passing fancy,
But the peace of eternal goodness,
Like sunshine through a cloud.

I would like myself to be one,
Not with beauty, vain and proud,
But everything still or moving,
In this and every nation.

I would like my love to flow out,
Not like milk, just here and there,
But a thousand rainbows rampant,
Encompassing all creation.

The 'Now' Quest

This wild imagination
curiously loops back and forth,
Across the one way passage of time,
And collects in each encounter,
With the path of happening,
A residue of perfection denied,
Salvation unfulfilled.

In the misty future,
These loops of the mind,
Create the cores of Time,
And being untamed, they are many.
Till reality intrudes,
And all is past.

In between the two,
The here and now,
Is neither here, nor now.

- So man lives
And so he dies

ᴓᴓᴓ

Om

When the clouds form,
On the distant hills,
When the breeze is cold,
In this desert land,
Again and again,
The mind repeats,
Om!

ઉૹઌઉૹઌઉૹઌ

Life & Death

I meditate upon,
The impermanence of life,
And of death.
I find myself lost,
In this and that,
Logic leaps,
Grasping and firm,
It is but,

The logic of life,
pale in death,

When the mind is still,
I reach a veil,
Beyond which, all is dark
Or bright - who knows

I am sure,
in a simpler world,
What we call life & death,
Would be but one.

We are Forever

When I write peoms sweet,
When I sing the song sublime,
When I do a kind deed,
When I whirl in no-time,
I can shout, like you, Mansur,
“Ana al Haq” - I am the Truth.

Let them kill me too, if they will.
They know not, deluded ones,
We are Forever!

Wonderworld...

I have glimpsed a world,
Where time is not,
And clocks are just, decoration pieces,
From a life gone by,
Going on…and yet to come.

I cannot explain any better than that.
Alas, I came back, all too soon.

Idols

I am an idolater, yes,
But have you seen my idols?

Anchored images of tranquillity,
On the sea of existence,
The loving kiss, of deified bliss.

Like spiritual lenses,
They focus my senses,
Onto the divine,
On your God and mine.

Come and see a world apart,
In the temple of my heart,
Where all is as it should be,
Between my idols and me.

Awareness

Like Narad,
I do not know myself,
Though I have read everything,
From Vedas to snake charming,
From Sloan to Samuelson.

I continue to surprise myself,
By my Self.

ઉઝઊઉઝઊઉઝઊ

The Interlude

Lines on the palm, bent, to let in fate,
Often Devil's fence,
sometimes heaven's gate.
Happenstance misting the course of life,
Will changing destiny lying in wait,
Roiling waters lived in a storm,
Of happiness and sorrow, love and hate.

That is life, mine and yours,
A short stay and back indoors.

ന്ദ്രന്ദ്രന്ദ

My Song Eternal

I need a clock, with a luminous dial,
That my tired old eyes can see,
How much of the night remains.
I have tried to count the ticks,
But with each tick, a memory comes,
Making me wider, and wider awake.
Yet what is gone,
Is gone forever,
And now I wait, with bated breath,
For it, to ebb away.
When I die,
Take the fire from my hearth,
And let it consume me,
That, which kept me alive.
I will be born again and again,
And yet again, till infinity,
Or till I need the clock no more.

Half asleep…

Patience and faith, my Gurus have taught,
To look past that which I am not
To go where arises this inner laughter,
And become one with it, ever after.

My quest is unusual, I seek what's here.
To become All, without all that's dear.
No rituals I need, no minarets or tower,
I'm a lotus bud, waiting to flower.

And, if you only knew,
So are you and you and you…

My Poems Write Me....

I do not write my poems.
Emerging from my heart,
My poems write me,
Word by word,
Line by line,
And, in their work,
You can see who I am,
A picture clearer than any artist,
Or camera could have captured.

Recognise me not,
By the form you see, with your eyes,
But from my words,
Born in my very core.

ᘓᘏᘓᘏᘓᘏ

I

I, too, was a unit of light till I came to this earth,
And now the light in me, is too deep to see.
I get glimpses of it in my gentler moments
Sometimes when I sleep,
And my senses retreat,
But mostly, darkness swirls upon darkness,
In deepening shades of grey,
Till the blackest black,
Of violence is reached.

Dark is unhappiness,
                    and happiness too,
For it traps and leads one away.
Of these two the shade is made,
Which hides the light.
Coiled in me are springs of emotion,
These create glory and glamour out of the gross,
And sorrow and grief, too
                    - not much different.
Through fire and ice,
Through love and hate,
Through this world and that,
All changes,
                    but that spark in me,
Life itself.

ଔଔଔ

Destiny

There is a moving ladder we try to climb,
From the commonplace to the sublime,
But the ladder moves at its pace,
And forces a look at destiny's face.

Yet, our efforts are not unseen.
There's always someone & has been,
Who moves the ladder up and down,
And watches us laugh and frown.

So try on and do your best,
Be sure destiny will do the rest.
It's not random fancy or whim,
We shape it by what we do for Him.

ଔଷଔଷଔଷ

Silence

Step into my silence, softly,
For here, undisturbed by thought,
The Eternal lives.

Leave you loves, your hates, your fears,
With your shoes, at the doorstep,
And bring into my silence, not a whisper, No,
Not even your name, your body, mind.

No hymns are here, no sacred chants,
Reverence was, but is no more.
Incense, sacrifice matter not.
The path has ended at the door.

Here is no name, no label, marque,
That brands you, you, and me, me,
Here, all are one, and one is all.
Come, atep into my silence, softly
And see, that I've always been you,
And you, me.

ଔଔଔ

The Promise

Saffron whispers beckon,
Softly, insistently,
Come, close your eyes,
And see the light.
Choose one fulfilment for another,
A promise of nothing for no-thing.

ঔঌঔঌঔঌ

The Way

There is little I can say,
That adds in any way,
To what's been said before.
I have travelled far,
But the remaining miles are,
Many, many, more.

ເສຣ໋ເສຣ໋ເສຣ໋

The Eternal Joker

Dreamer I am, through and through,
I dream a me, and dream a you,
I often dream worlds anew,
And all think, they really are.

No logic lives, no minutes march,
All is <u>now</u>, no future, past,
I make things, that will not last,
And games are played,
Of zero sums.

Life and death pass me by,
In bridal veils, hesitant, shy,
I make them laugh, I make them cry,
And go on,
My merry way.

Of Hope Undimmed

I have waited long,
In this darkened place,
But I sleep not lest I miss,
Those dainty steps, that beloved face.

I wait, and waiting in me,
My music sleeps,
Its strings wet with unshed tears,
Its flutes but exhausted reeds.

The dancing bells have closed their eyes,
And arm in arm they lie aside,
But I wait with bated breath,
For I am sure you said 'tonight'.

My song that was, is now a hymn,
Even the grapes are now old wine,
This bed alas, an unfulfilled altar,
But the dawn is not yet,
Beloved mine.

Heartfelt

In the centuries I have lived,
I have seen many stages of life,
Each marked by love of a kind.
Much of the time it was of the body,
Sometimes, of the mind.
Now that it has touched the heart,
None can tell,
Love and lover apart.

ଔଔଔ

A Dream Divine

An angel passed over me, as I slept,
And I dreamt a dream divine.
The light from its halo fell on my body,
And it was no longer mine.

My heart was for those who cared.
My arms were for those who dared.
My eyes were for those who saw,
The helpless and the weak.
And for those who could cry no more,
I gave my tongue to speak.

And so on the glow spread,
Till on everything it did shine.
At that moment I was the world,
And the world was mine.

The Tao

There's little I can say,
That adds in any way,
To what's been said before.
I have traveled far,
But the remaining miles are,
Many, many more.

Alas

On the cusp, a beautiful moment smiles
bemused and moves on with its promise
of poetry, in a life of prose.

Emptiness waits no more and, till the next
time, all is paragraphs again.

ঌঌঌ

The Truth I Am

My body, daughter of the earth,
Moves with the Earth.
My mind is a whirling dervish,
Dances a dance of ecstasy,
Faster and faster, till an eddy forms,
And all escapes, into nothingness,
Leaving me, in a place beyond words,
The body forgotten, the mind drained.

All is still, and, in the utter calm,
The universes, silently, expand in me,
As All-That-Is becomes,

All I AM!

Understanding

Whose tears form the sea of sorrow and joy?
Who is the boatman that I employ?
When I go seeking the holy grail,
Who's the breeze in my sail?

Who creates the storm and the tide?
Who's my pilot, my travel guide?
Whose is this boat that I'm on?
Where will I be, when it's gone?

There are no answers in my mind,
And till it's still and I go behind,
Where hides what I want to find,
I'll just keep on sailing blind.

Many books have had their say,
Now words are shoals in my way,
To go beyond this stormy sea,
From all concepts I'll break free.
Enter my silence and there, see,
All the Three as only ME!

An Invitation

In Shav-asan, after a sojourn with the Self,
I lie, still as a corpse,
And often, in a heartbeat,
My arms open wide,
Quite by themselves, inviting the world,
To come and share,
My One-ness with it.
I know one day it will listen,
And I will then,
Be whole forever.

ଔଔଔ

Welcome to my Tavern

When religions make my heart bitter,
And my mind is in turmoil,
Music is a my safe refuge,
And wine a useful foil.

You too definitely are,
Welcome in my tavern, any time.
The music here warms the heart,
The wine is truly sublime.

Do not go by outer signs,
They are there just for show.
Here lies the secret of unparalleled bliss,
No 'sins' are here, joys grow.

Those who are close to the devil,
Will see devils everywhere.
Only divine light floods my tavern,
Come in, there's plenty to share.

Sophia Perennis was discovered here,
The vintage of a drunken heart.
When we are truly high on it,
We can't tell each other apart.

Stop preaching and come and see,
What Eshoa' really meant when he.
Spoke words to Thomas which set him free,
Of the difference between you and me.

I go in now and hope you'll too,
Have the courage to come in my dears.
My tavern's full of good old wine,
Let's go in and say "Cheers!".

ଔଔଔ

The Bitter & the Sweet

The universe will smile,
It'll frown,
Offering rags,
Rarely a crown;
However unfair this may sound,
As an actor I must meet,
Both the bitter and the sweet,
And greet them all, as a treat.

My script has both,
In my role,
They're needed
To make me whole.
Eavesdropping on the Eternal,
I know this as the Soul.

I know this as the Soul

ଔଔଔ

The Awakening

I would sing if I could,
But pure silence rules my mind
The path has ended at the door,
And I have left the gods behind.

Now every single day is holy,
Every breath, a mantra sublime.
I am nothing and yet......and yet,
I am ALL at this time

ଓଃଓଃଓଃ

My Life & Times

Awake at night,
Wondering what could've been,
Traveling different paths, seen and unseen,
And then, and then, the best feeling for me,
Knowing where I am is where I want to be.

Sweet sleep again,
Dreams known and unknown,
Some weird, but happily,
All entirely my own

And then the dawn,
Another smiling day…

ଔଔଔ

I want to wake me in you!

I want to wake me in you,
Just so that I'm there, day & night;
And inside you, you'll always know,
Nothing'll be dark in my light.

I want to wake me in your heart,
So when there you see my smile;
My warmth will spread to every part,
And you'll forget the world awhile.

I want to wake me in your mind,
Where thoughts arise, good & bad;
With me there you'll find,
You need never again be sad.

I want to wake me in your soul,
So that when our lives are done;
Both of us will remain whole,
And dance together as one.

CBSOCBSOCBSO

Fana – Almost There…

I donned the saffron robe,
And roamed here and there.
I begged from door to door,
And didn't get, anywhere.

I counted a million beads,
And recited every prayer.
I read all the books,
And didn't get anywhere.

I discussed God and Satan,
And all religions threadbare.
I fasted, days and days on end,
And didn't get anywhere.

Then wisdom smiled on me, one day,
And told me, in its own calm way.
These are traps of your mind,
Which you have to leave behind.

Just go inside if you want to find,
What is it that makes you blind.
To what is illusion and what is true,
To the false and the real you.

It spoke of power and it spoke of pelf,
It spoke of mind, it spoke of self.
It spoke of the real, it spoke of show,
It spoke of what I needed to know.

Now I fast not, nor do I pray,
I go nowhere but travel in a way.
And find the Truth, as wisdom did say,
Inside myself, at work and play.

It's not "holy" in the worldly sense,
It needs not knowledge, smoke, incense.
It's not demanding of ritual and fast,
It wants nothing that will not last.
It's "All-That-Is", never surpassed,
My future, my present and all my past.

Getting there....

Beyond shape and size, large and small,
Unaffected by water, earth or fire,
I am nothing, I am all,
Without attachments, without desire.

In silence I sit with those,
The few who understand.
No prophet am I, no god,
Just a son of this ancient land.
I go back to my ancestors,
Knowing, calm and wise.
As they were, so am I,
Just my 'self' - no surprise.

I am not what you see,
This fleeting body, fickle mind.
I am not my hopes and fears,
I have left those behind.

Shorn of all that I am not,
Like the sun in a cloudless sky.
In the quiet of the self,
This eternal soul am I.

An eddy in the ocean, I am,
Well-defined, but the ocean true.
Pure gold in ornaments fine,
That I am, and so are you.

The Sanatan…

I am a swimmer in the infinite,
Watching myself, sswim in me.

Sometimes, I laugh out aloud,
At who, I had been told, God was,
When I was a novice,
Reading my books,
In the classroom called life,
Preparing for exams,
Which were never held,
In compulsory subjects,
Dictated by others,
And options of my own choosing.

Then I found, the finals were just,
An interview with myself,
With me,
As the examiner!

The venue was not far,
Within myself,
But giving up my books,
And forgetting all I had learnt,
Took a long time.

Then finding my Self,
Did so too.

But now,
I am a swimmer in the infinite,
Watching myself swim in me,
Sometimes,
          laughing out aloud,
At who, I had been told,
God was………

ઉજ્ઞઉજ્ઞઉજ્ઞ

The Tree God and Me

There was once a Tree god who was alive,
I was sure. Every time I passed by, she shook
a bough & told me so.

She wished me well, for off and on, a fruit
would fall at my feet or a bird sing just for
me, in an angels' voice, soft & sweet.

She sheltered me from the sun. In the rain
I would run, under her umbrella, safe &
sound. I never worried with her around.

My exams always went well, when I bowed to
her on the way. She granted small wishes.
I just had to say.

Then one day, they cut down the tree and
took it away, leaving me alone, with a forlorn
bird, which sang no more, both of us, not at
all sure, how the world would turn out to be,
without our god in the tree.

Full of grief, I sat alone and a voice
whispered on its own, "Worry not, I'm
here, where I always was, my dear. You just
saw me in the tree, for you thought there's
where I should be.

In your heart is where I dwell, now, and in
the past as well. The bird will find another
tree but you'll always have me as close to you
as I can be.

I believed what I heard and I sense her day & night, but when I see a tree cut down, I still hurt inside, and think of the bird who I never saw again.

ઉઙ્ઝૐઉઙ્ઝૐઉઙ્ઝૐ

Varanasi

I met a man in Varanasi, in a narrow lane,
Eyes like lamps in the dark, alit, in a leonine mane.
He sat by the wayside, on the ground, reading an ancient book.
As I passed by, he said something, and stopped me with a look.

I stood in silence and he scanned me up and down.
Then he smiled a rueful smile, and slowly eased his frown.
He spoke and in his voice I heard the ancients of yore,
"You've been called many times, but you follow the Path no more."

"Look inside and you will see, if your actions are just and true.
You are here for a purpose, you haven't forgotten, have you?"
He spoke in Sanskrit and, to my surprise, I understood everything he said.
His words echoed loud and clear, inside my heart and head.

He went back to his Upanishad, I was rooted to the spot.
Memories came un-beckoned, of what I did and not.

I touched his head, it was a blessing, I sought from his matted hair.
Waves of love came to me, ending my despair.

Forgetting where I was headed, I turned back from this place.
I felt cleansed inside me, and awash in amazing grace.
When I woke in my bed, the grace was there to stay.
I remembered the old man very well, and what he had to say.

I know if I actually went there, I will not find him any more,
But he'll find me, when the need arises,
Of that I am sure.

ଔଔଔ

Patterns

Learning to talk, learning to walk,
The struggles of youth, then romance,
Followed by the mellowness, of spiritual calm.

First the dance of the body,
Then the prance of head and heart,
And, finally the warmth, of the soul.

My Gods and demons churning away,
Past the problems, past the riches,
Till the nectar, of immortality emerges.

Sagar manthan, repeated,
In fractal patterns,
Again and again, on many canvases

The toil of life, the foil of love,
And finally,
          ....finally,
The magic elixir

I tend the fields as the young grape,
Starts in my vineyard,
Ripens, and then,
Ends in my tavern,
Guided by the divine.

ଔଔଔ

My Own Devil

Many an angel came calling,
When 'twas the Devil I went to meet.
They tempted me with bribes of honey,
And other things hard to beat.

I said no, I wanted to see,
The Devil for myself and I knew,
God will agree, for after all,
He had made the devils, too.

They said he is evil, he is bad,
He will make me like him, impure.
I asked if they'd met him themselves,
And they said, "we have, for sure".

"Then you must know", said I,
"That my devil's not the same as yours.
Each one has a different devil,
Behind our names on these doors".

"And unless we meet our very own devil,
We'll not know who we are.
And that is why, my guardian angels,
You must let me go that far".

They did so and I went on,
To open the door with my name.
There I found wealth and pomp,
Envy, fear, shame and fame.

I kept looking half my life,
For the expected Devil, all my own.
Till Wisdom came one day and said,
He is only what you have sown!

ঙ৪ঙ৪ঙ৪

At Midpoint

If I could touch a cobra's venom, and turn it into honey,
If I could make a madman sane, or make death appear funny,
If I could pat a hungry lion, and make it walk away,
If I could make a blind man see, or make an atheist pray,

And then, if this makes me happy, and others full of glee
I haven't reached near the end, there's a long way left for me.

For most things already are, as they ought to be.
I can't write someone else's script, I can only see,
And play my part, the best I can, in Act Two of three.

ઉଷ୍ଠଉଷ୍ଠଉଷ୍ଠ

Consciousness

The tree trunk I am, the leaf that sways,
Firm & dancing in the sun's rays.
I'm the roots that nourish all.
I see myself, in the forest,
As the breeze & the waterfall.

The stones & soil, are me as well,
The very earth, which forms our ground.
I am it, and other things, too,
I am consciousness all around.

Why?

I prefer to sit and drink with a friend and recount my exploits, while my lover waits on the other shore.
I choose the familiar warmth of my body, the soft cooing of my mind, to what can be much more.

I mumble, and call it poetry, without thinking why.
Then applauding wildly, pat myself on the back, so drunk am I.
I stumble and think I dance like a ballerina.
I prance and preen & look around, while inside me, echoes my lover's sigh.

Being Special

I sat in the Gurudwara, rapt in respect for the
Guru, with humility of service, echoing in
me.
I heard the muezzins call and heard the
greatness of God, like many in the mosque,
I could see.

I stood in the Church singing psalms; the
compassion of Christ moved me to my root.
And cross-legged in the Mandir I merged
with my Krishna's flute.

In the Temple of the thousand lamps, Buddha
smiled at me.
Then, like Hanuman, I opened my heart, and
Ram I could see.

Amused, the Formless formed itself as Devi,
or whichever form I chose.
And in my ecstasy, I saw myself, in every
one of those.

Then, suddenly, no more games
In the quiet of my mind all forms dissolve,
And in the centre of my heart,
Radiating infinitely,
I see who I am.

My visits to these places,
Were needless, I could see.
The Divine sat smiling, all the while,
Right here, inside me.

ଔଓଔଓଔଓ

True Independence

The world may be an illusion,
Served by the devil's crew,
But till we live, you and I,
Will swim in this brew.

Let me show you a way,
Well-known but used by few,
And divulge an open secret,
Ancient, yet forever new.

Trances are a waste of time,
Holy bribes you must eschew,
Set aside your cap and robe,
And be a seeker true.

Rituals are not for those,
Intent on going through.
Or the rules of others,
On what to do, or not to do.

All thought is useless,
And the top-knot is, too.
Words lead you astray,
In the search for YOU.

Let me add value

Let me add value to all the lives I touch,
Even if its only, one petal at a time.

Let me add poetry to all who hear me,
Even if its just, one meter or a rhyme.

Let me add peace to all I meet,
Maybe just a whisper, of the sublime.

Let me add love, to every frown I see,
Till it becomes a smile, even just a sign.

Let me be remembered, for giving myself,
To all who I am, and who are truly mine.

Rumi and Me

Why do you read Rumi? They ask.

All I can say is, beyond the ‘you-me’,
I am Rumi.
As proof I offer, his verses spoken,
Through my heart.

At times, we are Shams, our Friend,
At others, Qamar, and Najma, too.

And that is why the sun, the moon,
The stars twinkling in the sky,
And of course, Rumi and I,
Love reading our words,
Again and again.

Water Debt

You gave me this body,
But I owe no water-debt,
For I will not return,
That, which will harm you,
As it has, me.
For, was I not divine,
Till this ‘gift’ from you?

ଔଔଔ

Priceless Divine

Do not bribe your gods with sweets,
Bribe them not with future deeds,
Ask them nothing for a price,
Do not offer sacrifice.

You will get what you merit,
As per divine debit & credit,
Deeds you have done, thoughts thought,
Remember your gods cannot be bought,
Or else they'd be human, too,
Floundering around like me and you.

If you want something, by all means pray.
The Divine will hear what you say,
If it adds light to the day.
But if your wish is dark & full of hate,
Talking to gods is tempting fate.

Of Gods & Men

I touch the wrinkled brow, see the tired eyes,
And I remember a time, when God was young.
When She rocked me, in my cradle,
And, in Her smile I saw,
A thousand worlds, a-forming.
In Her face,
Countless possibilities aglow.

Then I grew up, She was older, too
Hand in hand we watched
As the Cosmos cooled.
And she said, "my son,
All this is yours, do as you will"

And now, I sit by her,
Galaxies slow their spiral dance.
Suns are hot no more.
Stars their twinkling cease.
As they look back where She lies,
Looking at them, in silence.

In silence
I touch Her brow,
And hear a chuckle,
From the cradle I rock,
With my other hand.

The Transition

When I hear seers inside my heart,
It dances to their un-sung song.
They beckon me from in there,
And gently ask me to belong.

Where all atoms answer to my name,
And love is but a shadow pale.
Mundane lives, but a game,
Ego-less, I'm not male, female.

Then the outer world beckons,
Where loud words have their say.
Songs have to be sung to be heard,
And I am back in this play,

Ruing what I could be,
The whole Universe, with all its wealth,
Instead of worrying about petty stuff,
And keeping my ego in good health.

The Olf Hollow at the witching hour

In the Olf Hollow,
At the witching hour,
You can become, what you want.
Wish - and the physical self,
Changes to your desire.

When the eastern wind blows,
Your inhibitions away,
When the naked self dissolves,
You may emerge sheep or wolf - but always,
What you want - that you are.

But beware!
Many things with the eastern wind,
Blow in, at the witching hour,
That were just shadows,
At the back of your mind.

Dark shapes and light,
                    parts of you,
Emerge alive and well,
When the inner self melts,
And forms you, anew,
In the image of who,
You really are.

In the seed of your dreams,
                    the germ of truth,
Is always there.
Step with care, if you ever dare,
Near the Olf Hollow,
For when transformed, you may rue.
The day your dreams came true.

ଔଔଔ

In this upside down world…

Some will mourn when I go.
They'll say, "I loved him so".
But I want you to know,
That's only how I'll grow.

I won't be in the realm of gods.
I won't be in heaven or hell.
Beyond the call of the muezzin,
The sermon of the priest, the temple bell,
I'll be with those truly mine,
Waiting for others left behind.

We'll meet soon one day,
To laugh together, plan a play.
New things to do, new things to learn,
Some prarabdha to earn, some prarabdha to burn.
And so our dreams will start again,
With another cycle of sun and rain.

Indeed,
This life's a dream, dreamt as a team. Yet when we awaken, others think we go to sleep forever.
Such is 'life' and such is 'death' in this upside down world.

Hope

When the suns are cold and the heavens dark,
When planets from their exertions rest,
There comes the song of a single lark,
Remembering all that was the best,
In the ancient music of the spheres,
Which through time slowed and slowed,
Till, quite unforeseen by the seers,
The Universe ends on a beautiful note.

At that moment, cold and dark,
Resting alone, undecided, unsure,
She listens a while to the lark,
And rekindles it all,
Once more!

❧❧❧

The Dream-Maker

My dreams are alive, and some of them talk.
Some of them smile, some grin, some love.
Some in vain pursuit, run here and there.
Looking for dreams of their own.

Some dreams, malignant and dark,
Mutate into nightmares,
And hold my tranquillity hostage,
At the whim of the Dream-maker.

Yes, it is She who rocks the cradle,
Where made of hubris, dreams are born,
And moulds them, She who knows best,
What I am, what you are

Me, Myself

When I lie awake, in my bed,
I think of things,
And I think of things,
Thinking for me.

Of such half-dreams,
Would my fears be born,
But I've been there & I have seen,
The musicians asleep, the laughter, resting.

Evocations of grandeur, of warmth and love,
At my beck and call,
I am sure there is a me,
Beyond chemistry.

ઉ઼ઽઉ઼ઽઉ઼ઽ

Dilemma

Inside the core of my being, someone asks,
Who am I, trapped in this mortal frame.
What makes me, ‘me’, and you, ‘you’?

With noises stilled and the mind blank,
A small hint of truth dazzles.
I return to the noises,
Sometimes with relief,
Sometimes with sorrow,
For I know not, what I want, what I love.

ᗧᗤᗧᗤᗧᗤ

Of the Spirit

I love, and with love as my thought,
I learn things that can't be taught.
My feet, they dance on their own,
And tho' just 'me' I'm never alone.

I know not the words,
But sing the song.
Yes,
This is where I belong.

ঙঙঙ

Some Whimsy, Some Magic

I would like a lavender ocean,
With gentle waves, crested with gold.

I would like two rainbows in the sky,
So that one can rest while the other shines.

I would like flowers of light,
With an afterglow in the night.

I would like a falling star,
To keep with me, as a loving pet.

I would like the laughter of children,
Playing afar, with pastel butterflies.

I would like unlimited forgiveness,
And nothing at all to need it for.

I would like and aura of peace,
Beauty and warmth, a tranquil permanence

And then I can say In my magic world,
"I am man,
In the image of God!"

An Epitaph

I am a chrysalis,
Waiting to be a butterfly,
So why cry,
When I go.

Death comes but once,
But once it comes,
We fly by passages diverse,
To other worlds.

But we will meet again,
You and I,
Who loved and cared,
We'll meet again.

We'll meet again.

ଓଃଃଓଃଃଓଃଃ

I am Time

I am where the wind blows across the Prairie,
And I am where snows cover the hill,
Where tears wash out grave sorrows,
I watch the crying, completely still.

I move not, nor have ever passed,
Yet all measure me going by,
As still, I hear them moving past,
The trilling laughter, the sibilant sigh.

You know me not, though I am here,
Silent, unmoving, calm, sublime,
As you rush by, often confused,
Calling me your Father Time.

You thought the Sun moved and you were still,
Till someone discovered what was true.
So it's with me, as you pass me by,
Convinced I am moving and not you.

Your Seers know this and they have said,
In the 'real' world, Time is not,
But they don't mean I am really dead,
Just, not 'passing' as you thought.

Of Truth & Lies

We are all connected by many ties.
Some are true and others, lies

In your lives, you can be sure,
True ones, pure, will endure.
But those of lies, under stress,
Will only cause you distress.

So look into each other's eyes
And learn the nature of your ties.
Make sure that they're made to last,
Before you let them bind you fast.

If they make you less than you can be,
If they do not leave you free,
Break them and do not rue,
For such ties aren't good for you.

If they make you more than you are,
If they make you feel like a star,
Bind them close to your soul.
They'll always keep you whole

Yes,

We are all connected by many ties.
Some are true and others, lies.
Wisdom is in taking care,
Which ties you opt to share.

ଓଃଉଓଃଉଓଃଉ

Me, the Ex Shape Shifter

A Shape-shifter I was,
With built in masks,
Different ones for different tasks
But as I mellow, in years & heart,
I cannot see many apart.

The friend peeps, from the father, no less,
And agnostic grandfather says 'god bless'.
The lover smiles with the husband's face,
Yes, youth now wears the mask of grace

Shape-shifter I was, but that day is done.
Increasingly, I'm the same for everyone,
And on that day I now dwell,
When I am the same for me as well.

In Praising You, Lord...

In praising you, Lord, I paint you with words, golden and glorious, the best I have. Many word-strokes later, I look back at the letters, commas, exclamation marks and their kin and realize till the full stop, all the ink was a waste, a conceit of my mind. I see you only where the canvas is blank.

In praising you Lord, I sing solemn songs full of devotion. Piety unparalleled. Listening, I find you are only in the silences between words and in the calm when the singer rests.

And yet, Lord, I keep glorifying you in words and singing your praises on and on.

I know not who I am and behave as if you know not who you are.

In the River of My Life

I started out in water,
Too shallow to swim in.
See me now, midstream,
In the river of my life.
There is laughter unbound,
With my dear ones around,
Living with me this dream,
In the river of my life.

I often watch with a smile,
Events rise dolphin-like, awhile
And end, smooth & serene,
In the river of my life
I am sailing in a place,
Full of amazing grace,
Because of how you have been,
In the river of my life.

Thank you, all.

ഗ്ഗ്ഗ

Waiting for the Seventh Stage

This strange dawn fills me with light and I
can see there's no difference between you and
me and that yonder tree is Us too.

On my lit stage, now I find, pointless tasks,
behind myriad masks illusions fine made by
me, all just mine.

As I experience beyond understanding, a
magical time, the mundane becomes sublime
and wonderstruck I wait for noon

'THAT' has gone, 'AM' has faded and
ego-less, past sane & insane only 'I' remain,
to disolve soon.

Burnt Offering

My ego, the progeny of my wandering mind is like Isaac to Abraham.

When the soul tells the mind, "Take now thy son, who thy lovest and offer him for a burnt offering," it's no surprise, that only for the wise, this comes to pass, and their Self, unmasked, shines, in all its glory.

For most of us in this looking glass, the mind stays away from the mountains of Moriah. It just laughs and goes its merry way, and our ego lives to fill our world, with its children, who shape our lives in its own image.

Alas, for us, our soul remains just an incipient God.

CBSOCBSOCBSO

A Wish and a Prayer

Send me no twilights, lord.
Lengthening shadows are not for me.
When the outer sun fades and darkness looms,
Pray set my inner sun free.

With it I will chart my path.
In its light I will dwell.
By it I will incinerate this world
And then burn heaven and hell.

Till naught remains
But consciousness pure,
And in its light I can see,
That All-That-Is is really Bliss,
And All-That-Is is really me.

ᘛᘚᘛᘚᘛᘚ

Just enjoy the play

The brain itself has no pain cells
But when the heart aches, it says,
I hear you, friend.

When fingers meet thorny tips,
When sighs are heard from tired lips,
When the air smells of fear at night,
When the eyes see the world a mess,
When the tongue tastes a rancid bite
The brain feels the pain no less,
Than its agents,
Keeping the world alive,

When the taste of good, mellow wine,
Or a loved one's thumbs up sign,
A ballerina's dance
Or a loving glance,
Lifts the heart, or music soft,
Blesses the ear, the brain is there
Relishing each sensation.
The wise watch this play
Of the body and the brain,
With a light touch, an amused smile,
Knowing well that after a while,
Both will be gone, and so too this world.

Only they'll remain,
And what they learnt,
This time around.

They know that they can't
Drink the water of a mirage.
They just enjoy the play,
While it lasts,
And wait for the next one,
Another day.

Of Our Life, the Self and the Mother Soul

People talk as if the body contains the soul.
It's almost like saying, a small part contains the whole.

Souls are vast beyond our ken. They don't stop where our bodies end.
A small part animates our lives as we play a game of 'Pretend.'

This game starts with a plan, all thought out before we're here,
But when our minds dictate our lives, they do things they find dear.
Busy with our lives, we are ruled by our emotions, desires & thought.
The Self watches & often prods us to its original plan that we forgot.

But engrossed in our Kurukshetra, between Pandavas and Kauravas, our very own,
We heed not these gentle reminders and surely reap what we have sown.

And so Prarabdha is born and attached to us.
The Self carries it from birth to birth,
Filling and emptying with our deeds, from hearth to pyre, pyre to hearth.

Some call it Karma and think it writes our very lives in words of stone,
Without remembering we are the author and the eraser – yes, we alone.

Till this Prarabdha has anything at all, we're born and die, to be born again. Filling it by our selfish deeds, by our ego, by being vain.

When we listen to the soft voice of our Self, its plan gradually appears nearer. We live our lives as we should, and our destination becomes clearer.

When we think less of what is owed to us, and more of what we owe the world, Prarabdha reduces on its own, and we march, flag unfurled.

Towards the day when this bag is empty, the soul-part, we call our Self,
Passes back to our Mother Soul devoid of all power and pelf.

No more lives to be lived, no more births to contend.

That is where this continuing drama eventually finds its blessed end.

The Mother Soul finds learning in our lives. It finds fulfilment and even fun,
As it moves towards the hoped-for future, where the soul and Oversoul are One!

❧❧❧

Let me dance all my dances…

I'm just a witness here, witnessing the active 'me'.
Why do I do what I do? Why do I see what I see?
This 'why' the eye can't espy. This 'why' the mind can't find.
The mirror echoes it back to me. I must try to peek behind.

This is easier said than done.
This is not an easy quest,
Even if I was the owner here,
And I am here but a guest.

But wait,

My revered Guru is near,
Gentle, wise, infinitely kind.
He whispers in my eager ear,
A secret that he's divined.
In the stillness of no-mind, lies the answer to the 'why'.
That's where I'll find, the secret of the "I",

But there’s a catch, I’m told, to live there, I must die,
And let go of worldly gold, cut my head ere, I fly!

So many riddles so much fear, such a heavy up-front cost,
To find the ‘I’ that’s so near, the one they say isn’t lost.

I beg abashed, ‘forgive me, let me live this life of mine,
Being as good as I can be, before thinking of being divine.

Let me dance some more dances, let me sing my last song.
Let me laugh with my friends, ere I go where I belong’.

A vision, perhaps from a past life…

On a moonless night, on an ancient
mountain, in a holy lake. Still like a mirror,
I see the Milky Way, from where I came and
where I'll go, when this dream is done.

I look down entranced, at the stars.
They speak to me of belonging.
Suddenly, unexpectedly, a single drop falls on
the water, rippling the image.

A tear of joy, from my heart overflowing with
love, to my home. patiently waiting.
From a reflection, to a reflection, both moved
one way and another.
One whispering, 'I am yours' The other, 'We
know!'.

On the far shore, I hear a bird softly sing
Perhaps it, too, kept awake on this enchanted
night and is waiting, like me, to fly away....

ఌఌఌ

Celebrating Death

When I think of death to come, I see a
cheerful, flower filled door swinging open -
loving smiles, I want rush in there once more.
A warm welcome, where wait those I loved
and who loved me. Some I knew this birth,
some past on earth and air and in the sea.

Many births in many forms come alive in
me, beyond this life. Strangely, only love is
there, no negative thoughts, no wasteful strife,
no skulls, no scythes, no fanciful fires of a
childish hell, nor rivers of sticky milk and
honey, no judging God, no tolling bell.

Just sparkling life, wiser than before I was
born on this plane, amazingly free, full of
wonders. No mind to worry, no body, strain.
And creativity - far beyond magic, whatever I
think, I make appear. I can go wherever fancy
strikes. There are no walls, there's no fear.

In the gross world where we are, cry not for
me, you and you. Your loved ones are also
beyond that door, and I will be there waiting,
too.

ꕥꕥꕥ

Mars

Ares, Auqakuh, Bahram, Harmakhis,
Her Desher, Hrad, Huo Hsing,
Kasei, Labou, Mars, Ma'adim,
Maja, Mamers, Marte, Mawrth,
Nirgal, Al-Qahira,Tiu,
Simud, Shalbatana,

Always Mangal, waiting, watching,
For aeons, orbiting near.
Reflecting the colour of blood that flows
In the name of God here.

ଔଔଔ

A Passing Thought

Some mornings, I stand at the edge of the day,
And try to see the other end.
Often, in the thick of it,
Surprises wait at every bend.
Sometimes I float above the world,
And find it a game of 'Pretend'

There are other swimmers here.
Some try to pull down all they meet.
All they want is the highest seat.
Some others I come across,
Are truly hard to beat.
I look forward to meeting them,
As a very special treat.

Others are here too who're nice to know.
I greet them from my heart, & not just for show.
Yet others live their lives, unheard and unseen.
It's nowhere they are headed and its nowhere they have been.

So it goes day after day, my life common and rare.
I'm sure you know what I mean, for I've often seen you there.

ଓଃଓଃଓଃ

Make no tombstones for me

Make no tombstones for me,
For I'll live on in you.
Just going to change my body now,
Will soon be back - good as new.

Let there be no rituals.
All these are past their 'use-by' date.
There's no way they affected my life,
There's no way they'll affect my fate.

Dates of life and death are pointless,
The dash between them was great.
It was a colourful, curlicued pattern,
The line, definitely, was not straight.

Some you shared, the rest I lived,
Boisterously, just in my mind.
Both dances were a lot of fun,
And fate, too, was very kind.

That's how I'd like to be remembered,
With lots of laughter, food and wine,
While I revel in blessed freedom,
In my other world divine.

Drown my joy in no tears.
No somber faces I want to see.
Do not feel sad, at all for yourself,
And never, ever, feel sad for me.

ଓଃଃ୨୦ଓଃଃ୨୦ଓଃଃ୨୦

Choices in Autumn

Alas, so many doors, which were misty, afar,
Seven decades later, welcome me ajar.
Each I'd love to explore, live life behind them all,
But how I wish, it were Spring, instead of Fall.

Like you, I too wonder….wonder and wait to see,
Ere Fall turns to Winter, which one will it be?

Will it be the Spiritual, full of silence and bliss?
Will it be the one with tender warmth, loving kiss?

Will it be the Social, my gift for my land?
Will it be the Political, with its noisy band?

Will it be the Scientific, full of logic, well writ?
Will it be the Clever, with its sly dry wit?

I think I'll opt for the warmth of love & laughter,
For in this, I know, I'll live happily ever after

But despite this comforting thought, other doors beguile night & day,

And, alas, undecided between them, I fritter my Fall away.

ଓ଼ଃଓ଼ଃଓ଼ଃ

The Spiritual Quest

The spiritual quest is a funny one. To die and then live on unfurled, to cease to be and be the world. To find God at one's beck and call. To lose all "others", big and small. This happens here to the successful traveller every day.

Answers to questions, oral or written, lead nowhere, and the unexplored path remains misunderstood, now and forever, till travel on our own, patient and sincere, brings us where we started from.

Unfortunately, when we travel, as is our wont, we carry our baggage along with us. We do it on this quest, too, but on this path, the turnstiles allow only those with no baggage from the past.

The longer we keep our baggage, the more our attachment grows and the more difficult it becomes to let go of it. Much has to be unlearnt, and, often, that is the most difficult part. The thought of leaving long-practiced rituals, chants and fasts, often tears us apart and we cling to these and stay exactly where we were, circling signboards instead of going where they point.

The spiritual quest is a funny one. The words of seers are often sublime. Yet, those who need them the most can't understand what the seers say. And those who can truly understand do not need these words to show them the way. We go to seers to show us the light and we end up worshipping them, or their words, while their grace, their wisdom, remains untouched.

Here a rock can talk and the blessed can bless soundlessly. A flower can sing the song of the divine and a fly can become as iridescent as its wing. The world can change in ways that surprise, and vision is here without one's eyes. We can fly and stay where we are and try to go here and there and reach nowhere.

Yes, the spiritual quest is a funny one.

A Wish

Consuming my prarabdha and my present desire,
I wish to burn like a steady flame, in a windless place,
Till neither is left, not the fuel nor the fire
And unveiled, I glow with divine grace.

The Bandmaster...

When I decided to experience this side, some others like Anger, Envy, Lust & Pride, also came along for the ride.

They have a master, wand in hand who conducts the symphony of this band. Preening, thinking itself grand.

It was small but slowly grew. Now it veils what is true. It draws the lines 'tween 'me' and 'you.'

It's my ego, it rules the mind. Pushing my true self behind, it makes me all that you can find.

But one day I certainly know it must be made to go and then you and I will grow into what we always are....

A Timely Wish

The past is only in our mind,
The future we still have to find.
Let's all be amply clear,
Only the present is present here.

This is where future turns to past,
It's momentary and doesn't last.
It keeps getting born anew,
This oar-lock for me and you.

Keep your eyes on the prow,
Watch carefully where you go.
Always be aware where you ARE,
Instead of past and future far.

May your oar locks remain strong.
May you reach where you belong,
And there,
Past the vagaries of fleeting time,
May you live in bliss sublime.

* Oar lock: When your oars find unexpected currents underwater, oar locks help twist the oar, reducing the chance of the oar being pulled from the hand. They also allow skimming the blade over the surface of turbulent water.

☙❧☙❧☙❧

Desire…

In the recesses of my mind,
Dark and bright fantasies abound;
Of beauty and health,
Of unlimited wealth,
Of love and peace
And everlasting ease.
So many others can also be found.

Now and then some even come true,
But others left behind,
Are born anew,
In new forms, when I do.

Once born, they must stay,
Unless I can find,
What really holds sway,
In the recesses of my mind,
And resolve it away,
Before I die.

To be Holy…

No rituals are needed or scholarly tomes,
Pilgrimages to cities or hallowed homes.

To be holy, this where you start,
Gentle eyes, soft words,
Helping hands, generous heart.

ଓଃଓଃଓଃ

When I really smile…

*Some mornings I know how the valley feels,
when flowers bloom and birds return and
there's dew on the leaves, not ice.*

*Some nights are like that too. Gentle breeze,
mellow & kind, silence sublime, in a world
that's nice.*

*I pause my life, and live awhile,
And that is when I really smile.*

ଔଓଔଓଔଓ

Yog' – the Becoming

In the dark, passions stilled,
Her eyelashes brush against my cheek
Nothing else stirs in my world;
This is the peace sages seek.

But their beloved is harder to please,
Till their passions,
Are stilled likewise,
And their love, is as deep.

Then their union with All That Is,
Fills them, too, with similar bliss

These two tales of love and love,
Are similar and yet not the same.
One speaks of 'darling', 'sweetheart', 'dear',
The other really speaks no name.

Mine is the 'equal to' sign in a sum,
Theirs is what they have become.

For Ramana Maharshi

In your speech Wise One, I seek my silence,
In your appearance, my disappearance,
In your presence, my absence,
In your vision, end of division

In your eyes, my mindlessness,
In its place, filling the emptiness,
Your blessed grace, and in it,
The ME, I am, radiant, pure,
Now and forever.
That is all, I can say no more

Paradise Lost

I go looking for the lotus and find bukhoor,
And oud, jasmine & rose.
I love them so – I stay entranced;
I can't have enough of those.

So alluring are they, so nice,
Nothing beyond can I see.
I am enthralled by their spice,
While the lotus waits for me.

Wondrous nights come and go,
And joyful days too.
Older I continue to grow,
But we remain 'me' and 'you'

ઉଷ୍ઉଷ୍ઉଷ୍

Who Laughs….

Who laughs? Some nights I ask when laughter bubbles up, unbidden, unlike any other,

Who asks? I hear in reply.

I pause and wonder, which answer is more important, the first or the second?

Then suddenly it dawns! Neither!

I dwell in the laughter and all questions vanish. In those moments there are no words and nothing else matters till the laughter fades and only bliss remains, to also subside when I return to the mundane.

Laughter, Sublime

When I laugh without reason,
The laughter arises in stillness.
Then I wonder,
Who laughs
And getting a glimpse,
Laugh some more

ঙ্গ

Me…

Who possesses me?

Who do I possess?

The answer, either way is NONE,

Who can possess that, which is ALL

ଓଃଓଃଓଃ

Words have limitations….

They're born in the mind, but it's only in its stillness we find, that, which has been there all along

**

This secret cannot be explained by any wordsmith. Words form sounds, and sounds, however well intentioned, cannot describe silence.

**

Know you this. The silence of saints is more potent than thousands of words preached by poseurs or millions of psalms chanted by the naïve.

ଓଃଓଃଓଃ

If Only You Knew....

When I prostrate in front of my Guru, you are happy, for you see what you expect, but, in truth, one body bends in front of another, and both know, it's just for show.

Real respect is soul to soul, silent, calm, whole. Body-wise, if I may, the closest I can say, is 'eye to eye', 'heart to heart', as I unravel, part by part, till nothing remains of who I was, going around, ego-bound.

And I find, beyond the mind, egoless, sublime, who the Guru is, in truth, and the 'nameless' that I AM. No prostration is needed, in this embrace, of the divine him and the divine me. Just belonging true, of who you think, as 'two'.

If only you knew, we are One, as are you.

If only you knew.
If only you knew.

ଓ෴ଓ෴ଓ෴

The Story of My Life….

I'm a tightrope dancer, balancing a pole, with my life at one end, and ME at the other.

I spend my life, doing what I must, without effort, as the earth moves in its orbit

Step by step, moment to moment, looking left & right, mind-ful and mind-less, at Einstein & Ramana, Matisse & Nisargadutta, Begum Akhtar & Mansour al Hallaj, my loved ones & ME.

Like Schrodinger's cat, I'm neither this nor that.

Finding laughter everywhere, sometimes laughing at my folly, at others, laughing at my fortune, often laughing at nothing.

And so I live on, in the silence amid the din, a wave in the ocean.

And so I live, till I live no more…

Born in a cage with an open door,
Day after day I pace the floor,
Loving my refuge and making sure,
I stay attached to its allure.

Despite assurances from those who flew,
The dread of change, fear of new,
The thought of 'leaving' you and you,
Keeps me away from what is True.

Wonders through the bars I see.
There's no lock, I need no key,
But heart and mind can't agree,
Which of them should be free.

The mind wants the status quo.
The cage is beautiful, it loves it so.
The heart though wants to go,
But the mind rules, it says 'no!'

And when the heart, confused, asks it why,
It whispers, "I don't want to die…"

ദ്ദേദ്ദേദ്ദേ

Finally…

In my rush thro the universe, there was never time to view existence with love.

Born of a supernova, I passed through fire without a shrug. Saw orbiting diamonds without desire. Crossed empty parsecs, with a yawn. Aeons passed, many nightfalls, many a morn on alien worlds, never home.

Binary stars, I saw aplenty, countless planets, bound, and some lonely ones, ice cold, just floating around. Shiva's dances, yogic trances, merited just passing glances. Many births I saw, many deaths too as I sped by, unmoved and then, my Guru, I met you!

Now I know, certain and slow, that the past is past and the present, all, as I revel in seasons changing from colorful spring, to beautiful fall!

ଔଔଔ

When The World Dies

It comes for all of us, that time when this world dies,
And we emerge unscathed on the other side, to our great surprise.
Sounds of sorrow fade away, all pain gone, body-less, sublime,
Beyond the logic of the mind, beyond mundane linear time.

A loss, is it? No, not at all. You greet soul-mates, old and new,
And wait for those whom you loved, who'll certainly be following you.

So mourn not a dear one, mourn not the passing of his light.
Be sure that, in a better place, it's still shining bright.

I can't tell you not to cry, for you weep for yourself too.
The life you lived is no more & you're not ready for living anew.

But cry not for him who's no more. He's just in another class,

And, as for these moments, you can be sure,
Like everything else, these too shall pass

ꕥꕥꕥ

My Inner Journey…

I travel in my mind off and on to find the foul and the fair.
I go to corners hidden away, tickling my neurons everywhere.

There's a lot of music here, Arab drums and tabla beats,
Arias & ala'aps with their magic. Jokes are there & other treats

Demons too are often alive, and authors with their paper & pen.
Goddesses dance once in a while, new ideas prance now and then

I find ego-brick walls plenty, keeping my thoughts from being free.
I break these all, wherever I can, for they stop me from being ME.

If I'm lucky, I sometimes find, a niche where nothing stirs.
No demons or gods, no love or hate, no mine or yours, no his or hers

And there……

Passions stilled, emotionless, without desire,
I sit in the centre of Incandescence

Till life beckons,
For time is not now.

I leave reluctantly,
One womb for another,
Which I had left,
As unwillingly before.

ଔଔଔ

Either Way

On this side of death are those you love. On the other, too, they wait for you, and in the middle, the magic gate, closed for now.

But either way, love awaits.

Unless you hate, then, for you, there are others waiting, too. Either way…

ઉ૪ઊઉ૪ઊઉ૪ઊ

My Many Worlds

In my heart a world exists, and in that world, thousands more. In nostalgic moments I often go, to one of many worlds of yore. I meet loved ones long gone by, see forks I didn't explore,and often wonder what life would be, if I could live it all once more.

Then bemused, I come back to my world, here and now, to deal 'live' with its why and how, in the only timeline that the laws of this world allow.

But I know that in many worlds, time and space obey my will. I can come down from a peak, before I even climb the hill. In these worlds in my heart, the divine and I are never apart.

And here I find, no false & true,

No old & new, no I & you!

ଔଷଔଷଔଷ

My Tenant & Me

My mind was a Devil's workshop but, I asked it to leave. Alas, his black-coated minions have obtained a stay, and now, in vengeance dire, he's hammering away day and night, while the heat of his fire, shapes my desire, as he wishes.

With the legal system in my land of the lie, sometimes for sale, often passed by a snail, the stay will be vacated only after I die

A thought on 1st January 2021

Who will seek me in heaven,
Who will greet me when I'm there,
Who will I seek out and greet.

I sometimes wonder, but then I think...

Why wait for heaven, why not make it here?
Why pine for something that's so near?
All that's needed for this, I'm clear,
Is a loving heart & a mind sans fear.

And today, on this year's first day,
I reach out to you, just to say,
"You are in my smile, at work and play
And in my wishes when I pray!"

ଓଃଓଃଓଃ

Spring…

When it strikes you, the futility of everything, you must fight, with all your might, to once again, make your life sing.

Of what use is your day, when striving has ended, no fun & play, in a world gone grey, where no sun shines, and hopelessness is King.

Autumns will come and go and winters with their snow.

Let your mind, be of the kind where now and forever, it's always spring.

An Epiphany - Waiting for Baqa

If the lily is one of the manifestations of the bulb, whose manifestations am I?
In my ceaseless journey, whose way-stations am I?

Not the sperm of my father or the ovum of my mother,
Not the embryo when these two came together
Not the bawling infant, helpless and weak;
I'm none of these, and I continue to seek.

The callow youth, unsure, half-grown;
The young man, with a family of my own;
The granddad, well-loved, loving, too;
All say, we're you & yet not You.

I look in the mirror, I look in my mind,
I search thoughts that I may be hiding behind
In vain are my rituals, the pilgrimages I do,
I search ancient tomes, hoping for a clue.

I close my eyes and realize, I'm 'not this', 'not this', 'not this';
I've looked everywhere, what did I miss?
I stop searching and in silence sublime,

A voice whispers, you're wasting your time,
Looking at these things mundane,

For something not lost is so insane.

The One you seek does not hide,
Yet you wander far and wide
You search as if looking for a brother
You are You, you are no 'other'

Till you keep thinking in terms 'two'
You'll never live the real You.
Forget places to which you ran
Your search must end where it began.
You must heed these words of mine -
Behind your masks, you are Divine!

The voice whispers and then is gone,
Leaving me excited though strangely forlorn.
I look around wondering, who could it be?
Suddenly I know, *The Speaker was Me!*

And at that moment, explosive, new,
I know the false from the true.
I look past my childish disguise,
And burst out laughing, in surprise
I sit awhile, then look around
Nothing has changed on the ground

But now...

Not for me pilgrimages galore,

Or visits to seers door to door.
I am All and All is Me;
I'm the ocean, the river, the sea.
Wherever I look there I am.
My holy land is where I am.

Waiting calmly for permanent bliss,
Sometimes, fleetingly, I feel all this!

ଔଔଔ

On the Path To The Beginning

In my mind I atone not for my sins,
For I know exactly what these words mean
In the here and now.
Instead, I strive to return to my infant state,
Unwinding my life, unlearning all,

Till a blank slate is what I am,
No sins remain, no good deeds too.
No "me" is there and certainly no "you".
Just thoughtless thought, for All-That-Is.
To bless with grace, in timeless time.
In that space-less place, I will attain,
The blissful "at-one-ment",
That I am dying for,
One thought at a time.

Slivers of my life

Each moment is a sliver of my life,
        shaved by time.
Some are crude, others sublime.
Many are soft like flower petals,
Some are hard, just cold metals.

Sometimes, deep in my mind,
Some of their whispers I find.
These are of many a kind,
Of love & loss, of ties that bind.

As I grow old more slivers are shed,
Some stay alive, others are dead.
Now nearer my core, I can see,
A glimmer of who I may be.

I wait eagerly for that day,
When the final sliver falls away,
And I am there, a witness no more,
Just ME - aware, timeless, pure!

I dance sometimes…

The unsung song I dance on, sways my body like a doll
Unspoken sounds enchant, my heart, mind & all.

Then other songs intrude, those of the mundane kind,
And like Pied Piper of old, pull me behind.

Back in the real world, seers wait for me a-smile,
Watching me on this stage, where I'll be for a while.

ଔଔଔ

The Dance, the Dancer & the Rope, too

Ask me what I have learnt,
And this will be my answer;
The preface and the end are one,
And in-between, the dreamlike dance,
Of the rope dancer.

Once I woke up during the play,
And found myself as the rope.
Holding up both ends was also me,
While I danced on like a dope.

Suddenly ended the song and music,
Suddenly ended the passing show.
The lights went on & I was ME
That's all that I know!

Between Being & Non-Being

I sway between being & non-being, both have their charm
Yet, I like non-being more for in its bliss,
I come to no harm.

Time doesn't rule – all happens on its own.
No guilt attaches, no karma is sown,
I'm for all and all are my own.

I yearn to stay here, of this I'm sure.
To be a free spirit, a hostage no more.
To remain timeless, serene, pure.

Yes, that's the state for which I pray,
But fulfilment is yet far away.
Life holds me close, it must have its say.
And, so,
Between being and non-being,
I continue to sway.

ঙ্গ৪৩ঙ্গ৪৩ঙ্গ৪৩

Aum....

I bow to you, my protectors, not only physically but with my whole being in gratitude, for all the gifts that I have received in this life.

I come in humility to request that your blessings continue for those who I love and who love me. And, for myself, too. May our lives be fulfilling and may your hand be on our heads for as long as we live.

I do not speak my wishes aloud. I just whisper them in my heart where I know you will hear me, for there you and I are never apart.

In quiet moments, emotionless, without desire, I have often felt your smile, in the centre of my being, and this has resulted in unbidden laughter that has come bubbling up, seemingly out of nowhere. These are moments of pure, calm, joy - very different in their origin and form from the happiness that I experience in my normal life.

Accept my love, my divine guardians and keep watching over me and mine with your benign gaze.

I know, in time, as your wisdom burnishes mine and I truly understand who I am, the scope of my awareness will expand to encompass all. When that happens, we will perhaps laugh together at my follies and at the reality of this Creation whose very essence, I feel, must be joy. At present, though, that day is far, and for now, this is all that I ask.

Before leaving, I touch my forehead to your feet, again in my heart, as I have done countless times in many births. Doing so, I can feel your affection pervading me. Its goodwill will keep me safe and fulfilled till I am with you again.

Aum....

My Favourite Place

I ask authors inside me to write a story, but they keep arguing over the plot. I beg poets here to compose a poem, some want blank verse, some others not.

Quiet! I shout and they cower away, as I go to my heart, to hear its say. Here I find, in silence profound, sans writers, creativity unbound.

Among lotus buds, luminous flowers, droplets on petals, after gentle showers, I find songs aplenty, poems divine, amidst the fragrance, powdery, fine.

I can't copy these, must leave them here. It's nature's law and it's clear. They can only be experienced, not even read, nor can I explain what is said.

But amazing they are, they make me glow, in a way, only a few can know. These are those, who can find, the way to their heart, past their mind.

Some call it Fana, some other names. We've no use here for these memes. There are no labels, no words, no sound, when I'm in here – and all around.

Now's not the time, but perhaps one day,
when I'm ready, I'll be asked to stay….

Till then,

I visit here once in a while
And always return with a smile

You can, too….

ଔଔଔ

Tao

I can explode like a scream, creating waves which stir the Subtle and, over time, fade in it.

Or

I can slowly harmonise my being with All, and at the end, be one with the Universe, a part of its song.

Going by the past and the present, I think my future is the second Tao.

ᗢᗢᗢ

The Real You

Love and tenderness in an open heart,
Bitter acrimony tearing you apart.
Peace and harmony in a still mind,
Bigotry and rage driving you blind.

What fills you when you're empty,
Defines the real you.
What fills you when you're full
Does the same thing too.

ꕥꕥꕥ

The Happiness I Seek

Though, indeed, it is most inviting, O Rumi, I seek not happiness thine.

For I am too human and at this time, I have no wish to become divine.

Along the riverbank, water whispers, wings of birds, murmur and flap.

Beetles scuttle below buzzing bees, leaves rustle, twigs snap.

In this world, firmly on the ground, I dwell in silence amidst the sound,

And wish I could feel, in my heart awhile, the happiness I've seen in a baby's smile.

There and Back

When I stroll in the by-lanes of my brain,
I often see lightening without clouds or rain.

On an ancient park bench old ideas chat,
Of how things were, of this and that.

A bit away, young ones play,
Yet to mature, waiting for their day.

Here and there, new ideas arise,
Sometimes slowly, often a surprise.

I find a temple where no one prays.
No idols or incense, just serene days.

Through an arch I see "All That Is",
Wondrous calm, lasting bliss.

But those who enter, return no more,
And I stand wondering, no longer sure.

I look back at the life that I'll leave,
Memories in doorways, things I believe.

I hesitate a moment, then turn from the
Divine,
Giving up "All" for what I love as "mine".

I walk past the benches - old ideas grin,
As I trudge back knowing – I, lose, they win.

Timelessness

Time was born and it'll die and it'll be born again, quite like you and I.

Linearly it will seem to go, when you and I both know, it is only fooling us.

Full of ourselves, we will live, sometimes in the now, at others, in the past,

Often in the future, thinking we'll last.

ઙ૪ઙ૪ઙ૪

No Last Dances

There is no last dance in life, except the last dance of all,
And I do not mean death by it; that's a comma, rather small.

We live on and on, our lives are just actors' roles.
We are not the parts we act, we are our very Souls.

The last solo of ours, is an eddy's final whirl,
Before the stream claims its own, and our very Selves unfurl,
In All-That-Is, and always was,
Dancing away divinely,

Then, now and forever!

The Sufi

He was a real Sufi but he never a whirled about. Nor did he climb any minaret and shout. But one day, in his gentle voice, he did say, "For being devout, all you need, is a heart, so drunk on love of the divine, that you can't tell you from me, or yours from mine."

"Only when that happens, your journey will end where you began, and you'll be back home, whole again."

ଓଃଓଃଓଃ

Idle musings ere I sleep…

Life has a few commas and ends in a semi colon, not a full stop.

And then, after a pause, the next part of the epic starts, a new life, with its own commas and, when that is done, its semi colon. And so it goes till one needs these stories no more.

After that, who knows. Perhaps after all these dawns, I'll realise that I am the Sun.

And I am back…

I reach the gate and the gatekeeper asks for my ID. She takes it and throws it in the trash bin. Then she asks me to enter.

I have a feeling of loss. I rush to the bin and retrieve my precious card.

The gatekeeper looks at me with sorrowful eyes and turns me away. I ask why and she says, "your ID is fake and we can't let you enter with it".

"Will you allow me in without it, then?" I ask,

"Of course", she says, "but there should not even be any desire left to retrieve your fake ID from the trash bin. Till that desire remains, you have not let go of your fake label. Once that desire goes, you leave the fake ID in the trash and never return to it".

She paused and added, "You will then see that there is no door, that you've always been here, and that you do not need any ID to be One of us."

I think awhile. Her words are confusing. The thought of letting go of my ID is not welcome. I clutch my ID and turn back, to wake up in my regular world, to tell you of my failure to let go of who I've always thought I am.

The Real

Let me speak in terms that may make sense, or not. For the Real is unreal to who I think I am, and it's ALL, to who I AM

ଔଔଔ

I seek your Blessing, my Guru…

A smile on my face, a heart full of love, head bowed in humility, I come to you, my Guru, in gratitude, for showing me the way to the magic garden, and there, sowing the seeds of my emancipation.

With your blessing, I've tended these, the best I could, and now, bereft of my ego, I stand here, a thornless rose in the presence of a Brahma-Kamal.

Fragrant I am, but still rooted in the land, yet to enter the enchanted pool, which transforms thornless roses into Divine Lotuses.

Keep your blessings flowing, I pray, my Guru, to me and mine, till I'm there, and become all that I can be - All That Is.

The Things I think about…

Does a photon, for light years, know why
it has to come rushing to me so very far,
and suddenly one night, as I gaze at the sky,
enter my iris, to show me a star?

Are we puppets of advanced beings,
just an experiment for them to see,
what neurons will do, given free will,
what's it they'll decide to be?

Is space full, as Bohm opined and in it all
the stuff that we find, and we, who we
think so fine are hollows, marring the
divine?

I have a soul or does the soul have me,
or am I the soul, and all I see; this bird &
stone & yonder tree? Will knowing this
set me free?

ꕥꕥꕥ

Time and Timelessness

For no one do I ever wait
Some call me karma, some call me fate
Some call me their Father Time
For some I'm harsh, for some, sublime

Everything moves with my flow
And I watch eons come and go
I've seen empires rise and fall
And learnt much through it all.

The most important isn't so deep
"As you sow, so shall you reap"
I know you all, and I write down
When you earn a smile or frown.

But now a secret I must tell
There's no heaven or hell
All that is, is right here,
In your joy, & in your fear.

And, one more thing I declare,
Though true, it's very rare.
There are some who've gone past me,
Their record's erased, I can see,

And in their Truth, they now find –
I'm just a fiction of your mind.

Strange

God owns all, you say
And yet, when you pray,
You promise him you'll pay,
If your wishes come true.

God hears all, you say,
Yet holy songs you play,
Very loudly, night and day,
What's the matter with you?

ഗ്രജ്ഞാന്

This Time Around....

Strange as it may sound but it's all too true.
I know the treasure of One, but stay on in the Two.
I stand on the ledge but don't want to fall.
I love my love for a few, over the love for all.

I've read maps aplenty, seen many a road sign.
I know All That Is True, yet won't reach the Divine..

At least in this birth....

ꕥꕥꕥ

Me, Then and Now

I was a sun once, orbiting my galaxy, consuming myself an atom at a time, waiting for my end, aeons hence; Then one moment, watching another explode, I wished to Be, and by the power of my thought, was born as Me.

Now,

Orbiting this life, stilling myself one neuron at a time, waiting to be free.

ঙঙঙ

As time passes……

You've felt the fire, you've tasted snow.
You've watered seedlings & watched them grow.
You've been of the mountains and of the plains below.
You've seen what life has to show.

Now,

Everything looks nicer, in your inner glow.
Your thoughts are wiser, life mellow.
As time goes by, and hours flow.
There's one more thing, you should know.

Let the pace not slacken,
Let the music not slow.
You've danced many dances,
There are many more to go.

You've danced many dances,
There are many more to go!

ઉઇઉઇઉઇ

In My Garden

I see the buds and I imagine the flowers
they'll be, reach back in time to remind them
of their future shape. And I wonder, if my god
images are trying to do the same.

If so, I must remove the clutter around them
and clearly see, how I am meant to be, when I
am meant to Be.

ଓଃଔଓଃଔଓଃଔ

Nightlight Of The Gods

I often feel my consciousness is the nightlight of the gods. They sometimes awaken, see all is well, then go back to sleep, till the day dawns and absorbs the nightlight, in its radiance.

My music now, seventy five years in the making…

My heart doesn't sing the songs of my youth.
Then I was busy with other things.
There was no time for music then,
Wondering what the future brings.

Three youths old, now I find,
Music in my heart awaken.
It fills my heart, it fills my mind,
It fills all, not already taken.

I swim in it, I jump and dance,
My thoughts soar on hidden springs.
I often laugh & jump with joy
When my dear soul sings.

If priests were to see me move,
They'd surely call me pagan,
For I dance to music sublime
Music they've long forsaken.
But my songs can exalt,
Priests, popes & kings.
I'm blessed at this age
For finding my magic wings.

Of Pindar & Ramana, of this life and that…

In my dreams I sometimes hear,
Wise words from poet Pindar,

"Having learned what that is,
Become such as you are".

In my dreams, I too hear, Ramana,
Who's always near,

"You're not your body mind,
Nor who you so appear"

Oh, you & I, we both know,
Pindar didn't mean it so
But both are right in what they say.
I've now to choose my way.

I'll follow Pindar's advice,
Find the 'me', first of all,
And doing so, I'll be free,
To answer Ramana's call.

Then Pindar's '*me*' that I've found
Will no longer be around
But it's important that I know
Pindar's '*me*' before I go!

For without it, who'll search,
Who'll say, I must fly?

Without it who will strive,
Without it, who will try?

Like the matchstick that burns itself,
Pindar's *me* is for me;
And when it's gone,
I'll be, transcendent,
Finally free.

ଔଷଔଷଔଷ

The Past, the Future and the Now

The Past

I found a breeze under my wing,
And knew it was divine.

I heard then my soul sing,
And felt the world was mine.

The Future

Many I loved passed from present to past,
I'll join them some years hence.
None of us are here to last
This I know, it makes sense.

I'll be '*he was*' from '*he is*',
Here, in a realm older than old,
Where all is true, all is clear,
And nothing's ever bought or sold.

I look forward to adventures new,
A re-vision of all I've learnt,
Assessing my lives, as I view,
Karma earned and karma burnt.

The Now

But enough dwelling on what's to be,
Let's get back to what's here.
I want all of you close to me,
I want all of you to stay near.

I love life, it loves me too
And has been really kind to me,
Helped by love from you & you,
As it was meant to be.

While I'm here I want to live,
Dancing in my mind, whenever I can,
Taking much less than I can give
And laughing a lot – that's my plan

You're in my bliss too,
Giggling with me, in my dreams,
Perhaps an illusion for a few
It's as 'real' as it seems

ɞɞɞ

Laugh My Love

Laugh my love, for this life is a comedy,
though it often wears, a sombre mask,
sometimes tragic, sometimes farce.

See some actors, behaving as if, they are
Kings in truth, and paupers bemoaning, their
fate for real.

All play roles, rosy or grey, in a drama
directed in such a way, that the audience
themselves, act the parts, so earnestly, that
they believe, with all their hearts that in this
fray, they really are, who they play.

And the script is a very rough plot, to be
fleshed out, by what the players choose to do.

No one knows what happens, when the role
ends, and the actor, moves out of the arena.

Where does she go, what does she do, before
re-entering the stage, if at all, in a new act,
clad in another costume, maybe playing a
man, this time around.

Yes, no one knows, where they have been
between their shows, though many sell,
heavenly meadows, in a place they haven't
seen, whose owner, they haven't met, though

they claim to be sure, they are his Brokers, holy and pure.

The gullible pay a commission and buy an 'abode' which the Brokers say, they'll get, after the play, and it'll be maintained, by the Creator, for their pleasure

It is a measure of the comedic that multinational organisations, complete, with evocative logos, compete around the globe with the sole purpose of selling their myths, to fellow actors, through ethical practices, which would land them in prison, if there were dealing in anything other than un-real estate, which they do not own, in an imagined land, they have not known, through fancy brochures, they have made, in the roles they have played, or even entry tickets, printed by themselves, to take us past, an imagined gate, which they've thought up, and none has seen.

Through cleverly crafted incentives and disincentives, they do well and laugh all the way, to the bank.

You too, laugh my love, at what we believe to be true, for it is a comedy, of epic proportions.

Only some witnesses, knowing this are at peace, dotted here and there, in time and space, they can be seen, hallowed, with amazing grace, and looking at them, we know, that they have been, where they cannot be seen by other actors, regardless of what the self-appointed brokers may say.

These seers true, are the only ones worth listening to. They claim no ownership and sell nothing, to me and you.

Till you are one such, laugh my love, like an infant, just arrived on this earth, who knows nothing off this play, who knows not how to atone, how to pray, what 'sin' is, what it is not, who is too new to have forgot, who sent him here.

Yes, laugh my love, laugh and play, the role you have, the best you may and, remember, whatever you do on this stage, there's no cause, to look for applause from where you came, regardless of what some Brokers may claim.

You are the actor, you are the audience and, strange as it may sound in this theatre, it is you, who's your own critic too!

Patterns

Learning to talk, learning to walk, the struggles of youth, then romance followed by mellowness of spiritual calm. First the dance of the body, then the prance of mind & heart and, finally the warmth of the soul.

My Gods and demons churning away, past the problems, past the riches, till the nectar of immortality emerges. Sagar manthan, repeated in fractal patterns, again and again on many canvases.

The toil of life, the foil of love, and finally, ...finally, the magic elixir. I tend the fields, as the young grape starts in my vineyard, ripens, and then, ends in my tavern, guided by the divine.

ꙮꙮꙮ

Once in a while…

Sometimes in my dreams, those who've died
come welcome, but unbidden.
I ask them, now and again, "we love you so,
why do you remain hidden?"

And they say, "this body mind that you knew
was for us a prison.
Free at last, we are ourselves. Beyond your
dramas we've risen."

"We love you too, have no doubt much more
than you know,
But we are free of worry and pain. Why do
you wish us below?"

"Our old mates are here, as you my dear, will
also be one day.
There's love & laughter, there's joy, what
more can we say?"

"Our only sorrow is to see you cry, thinking
we've gone.
You look so lost, you look so sad, you look
so forlorn."

"Act with courage on this stage before you exit, too
Then together we'll plan grand adventures new"

They sound so vibrant and so young & sure!
Quite unlike the old ones who I knew before.

I thank them for letting me know,
And awake gently as they go.
Then keep lying quietly awhile,
With a relieved happy smile.
Knowing that the end,
Is not quite so

ᗢᗢᗢ

Song of the Agnostic

His holy book to his right,
A mitre to impress, a rod to smite,
On his throne he sits alone,
Like he's God's very clone!
Prideful, the pompous priest presides,
Followers quivering as he decides,
Who's for heaven, who's for hell,
A secret only he can tell.

They think, these simple sheep-kind,
"He has my interest on his mind,
He'll intervene with the gods that be,
Take my sins & so save me".

Well hidden under vestments rich,
I see his greedy heart twitch,
As he's offered money and gold,
By those enticed to his fold.

And with a smile, looking benign,
He makes his simple sacred sign,
As he counts with hidden glee,
The fish he's netted in his sea!

ଔଷଔଷଔଷ

The Divine & Me: Brahmasmi

One day, idly, I asked God, "What are you,
beyond your name?"
SHe smiled at me gently and said, "You 'n I
are quite the same."

I looked at myself in the mirror, and I
couldn't understand.
SHe is perfect, formless, divine, while I'm
just a man.

She laughed and said, "Listen carefully, for
this is certainly true.
*I am perfect, formless, divine and, so, indeed,
are you*!"

"Your mirror shows the surface, weaving tales
of its own.
You're sure these are true, & Real stays
unknown.

"Beyond the mirror you'll find who you really
are.
Your ageing body & fickle mind will then be
far.

Your ego too won't be there, with its power and pelf.
Here you'll find, your pure, unadorned Self."

Now I only visit the mirror that's radiant in my heart.
In it, with wonder, I can't tell, God and my Self apart.

In the Fall

Brown leaves keep falling for Autumn is here. I sit bemused, watching them, wondering, how green they were, how green I was. And now they return to the earth, to their roots, as I will, to mine, in my own time.

Does the tree mourn its leaves? Do the branches rue their fall? I have spoken to all, and they say, "We never beg the leaves to stay. We do not fear the cycle of life, my dear. Come spring, our leaves will be born anew, and we'll be stronger, too, with one more tree-ring added to others we have collected in years past."

"You, too, are a tree like us, yet, most of the time you behave like a leaf, reluctant to leave the stem, which you know, is so willing to let you go.

The Truth I Am…

My body, daughter of the earth moves with the Earth. My mind is a whirling dervish, dancing the dance of ecstasy, faster and faster, in sublime silence, till an eddy forms, and all escapes into nothingness, leaving me in a place beyond words, the body forgotten, the mind drained.

Passions stilled, emotionless, without desire I sit in the center of incandescence. The breath is soft, the world is stilled, until…. Until…, an explosion, unexpected, unwilled.

I am no longer me, as All-That-Is becomes All-I-Can-Be. In that moment, to my surprise, I find, I AM paradise.

But time is not now and I leave reluctantly one womb for another, which I had left as unwillingly before, and you meet me once more, in my body, mind, wistful, unsure.

But one day, when the time is nigh, I will be that nova in the sky. Look up then and say, 'he dared to be, what he cared to be.'

ঙ্গ ঙ্গ ঙ্গ

Yes, I Can!

I can rue that I am young no more,
I can cry, "the world has passed me by",
Or I can shape what the future has in store,
And make it laugh, dance and fly!

People & feelings that weigh me down,
I can exile from my world.
I can change to a smile a frown.
And soar high, wings unfurled!

ଔଔଔ

Whispers from Beyond

I hear these whispers now & then, in moments sublime.
Where time does not exist, how did I use my time?

How many bodies have I been in, how many more do I plan?
How many times was I a woman, how many times a man?

Do those who I have been, keep watching what I do?
Will those who I'll be, lead me to the True?

How can I access what I've learnt, in many births past?
What do I need to now unlearn, how long will this last?

And at the very end, when I am one with the divine,
Would it all have been worth it, this silly game of mine?

When I hear these whispers, in moments sublime,
I smile and move on, biding my time.

For mine is not to ask why, mine is just to find,
Who I AM beyond my body and mind.

When I find what's not lost, I am very sure,
All questions will fade away & I'll wonder no more.

ଔଷଔଷଔଷ

Meditation

The Universe blinks out in a magic moment,
as I meditate on the point, just before it was.

When the final sliver vanishes all that is left,
is me! A dimension-less seed of all I'll be.

At that moment, I know, without a doubt who
I am, for there is naught else, in no-time

ശജരശജരശജര

Did you know?

*Did you know some fireflies are full of lies,
pretending to be what they're not, waiting for
the unwary, and some people, too, are much
the same.*

*Did you know, one can use, the palette of
words to show the world nooks and crannies
of a heart unfurled and many can find
themselves there.*

*Did you know, every poem was once prose
that soared, lambent, as it rose, far above
others, on its own.*

And did you know, you too can be one of those

Did you know? Did you know?

ઉજ્ઞઉજ્ઞઉજ્ઞ

On the banks of the Ganga One Evening - between Devprayag & Rishikesh

Light a lamp and let it flow in this sacred river, so others know, someone from somewhere, far upstream, sends them a gentle, blessed dream.

ↄↄↄ

My Will

I can rue that I'm not young any more.
I can cry, "the world has passed me by",
Or I can laugh and make amply sure
That my life ends on a high.

Let my grave not be hallowed ground,
Let me tell you what's my will.
Near a stream which sings all year round,
Bury me with a sapling on a hill.

ઉઘઉઘઉઘ

True Belonging

Let our bodies act out the social norms
conditioned in us, but know my friend, in
your heart, where it matters, the soul I am
greets the soul you are, as a beloved twin,
eagerly waiting when our bodies distract no
more with their
play-acting, and once again we are,
just what we are.

This body loves this body, and that, while the
Soul I am watches, amused.

Many moons pass, waxing and waning and
then one day, the Sun rises!

ଓଃଃଓଃଃଓଃଃ

Why can we not laugh in God's house?

There is God in a child's laugh and in an old one's toothless grin.
Then why can't we laugh in a temple? Why is gaiety such a sin?

Why can't I chuckle in a church, why should the mosque be grim?
Isn't it the house of my Father, and I'm there with Him?

Why must I dress so formal, for Him who sees my soul?
Why must I ape a diamond, when I'm still coal?

If I dance in these places, will my Divine mind?
Isn't He always joyful? Isn't He always kind?

Why confine Him to a building, when He's here & there & there.
My world is my temple, I see Him everywhere.

Closest to me, in my heart,
Sometimes I can't tell us apart.
And there, blissful, free,
I hear Him often, laughing with me.

He asks now & then,
"*Why are they so prim*?
I want joy unbound,
But all I get is grim!"

Bless me

Bless me, my Gurus, not because I am good
but because you are so, and I need your
blessings to make me glow.

Bless me, my Prithvi, not because I am
worthy, but because you, O Gaea are so, and
you are generous, as I know.

Bless me, my Surya. Heed my gayatri, revered
Sun, on your chariot of fire, Bless me and
fulfil my desire.

Bless me, my Chandra, you of ageless legend
and lore. I meditate upon you, O Moon, keep
my mind cool and pure.

Bless me, my Aakash, without asking why, for
that I cannot define. I just know in my heart
that you are divine,

Bless me, my Vayu, you, of many names, who
keep me alive. Bless me to succeed in all that
I strive.

Bless me all, for I am human and my mind,
keeps moving here and there and I often find,
that with your blessings I remain good and
kind.

Bless me, for in me, you will find I'm your very own. I am a but a plant all of you have sown.

Make me prosper, make me grow, make me a model you can show to the world with immense pride. I know I can't fail with you by my side.

Bless me….

ઉઙઽઉઙઽઉઙઽ

If I'm Asleep

If I am asleep wake me not, for I have years of dreams still undreamt, nestlings just below the conscious, humming their songs, practicing their dances.

Eyeing me with sidelong glances, waiting for their fleeting chances, they double my life and take me to lands, often wonderful, and far better than I've travelled while awake.

Forms

A wave crashes and thinks it's no more,
But it's still water, as it was before.

Forms change but inside, the gold remains gold,
As we grow from infant to youth, to old,

And then, formless, return to who we are…

ଔଔଔ

O My Soul…

O my soul, I know you can sing. I have heard you humming gently just before I sleep and, sometimes, in dreams, I have heard your songs in my heart. But I am not awake then, my dear, my senses lost.

Sing me a song when I am awake, to make me fly out of myself, soar in the sky, flapping my wings to the beat of drums, where angels dance and a mare can become a unicorn.

I don't want to look down upon my world. I just want to see who I am, who is me, spirit unfurled in a heaven all my own, experiencing things still unknown. And where love can take amazing form.

O my soul, I'll forget this world, for as long as you sing, be it a day or anything. I have waited long, to dance with the birds, on divine music & magical words, taking me above my daily storm.

O my soul, sing me a song of joy, that I can hear in my heart and in my mind, know, who I am beyond this world, who I can be when unfurled, my being open to everyone, loving, warm.

Sing my soul and make me whole….

Illusion

Asleep, I watch bemused as I live from one dream to another in my make-believe worlds. Complete with sisters and brothers, fathers and mothers, all dreaming dreams of their own.

One day we will awaken and you and I will laugh again, as One.

☙❧☙❧☙❧

Timelessness

Time is not, some well know.
The falling rain, the river flow,
The earth in orbit, an ember aglow, Ancient mountains, covered in snow,
As we stay or we go,
Where we must.
Now and then, in my world, I escape Time,
And then, sublime,
I'm like the falling rain, the river flow,
The earth in orbit, an ember aglow,
Ancient mountains, covered in snow.
No choice is there on occasions rare, no ifs and buts.
I stay or go where I must,
And, heavens bless, when, Timeless, I am one,
With what's to be done.

꧁꧂꧁꧂꧁꧂

Father Time…

The crude, the banal and the sublime
Eventually we are all food for Father Time

꧁꧂꧁꧂꧁꧂

You & I

Let our bodies act out the social norms conditioned in us. But know my friend, in your heart where it matters, the soul I am, greets the soul you are, as a beloved twin, eagerly waiting for that magic moment, when our bodies distract no more, with their play-acting and once again, we are, just what we are.

ঙঔঙঔঙঔ

On Guru Purnima

From his eyes his gentle grace,
Peace in my heart from his smile.
Past the world and its manic pace,
I want to be with my Guru awhile

My Upanishads and Me

The Upanishads echo in my genes and I dance to their tune.
I know some of what this means and will know the rest soon.

In these there's a magical world, a place quite apart,
That'll still the turmoil in your mind & glow in your heart.

Just close your eyes & walk awhile, in their wisdom, timeless, true.
In ancient words, without guile, you'll find the real you.

Isha Upanishad (Yajurveda)

I take a strainer every night & pour my emotions in.
The pure I place in my heart and dross in the bin.

Kena Upanishad (Samveda)

As I greet the rising sun, to my gurus I humbly pray.
I thank them for all that's done & am ready for the day.

Katha Upanishad (Yajurveda)

Like Nachiketa, I visit death, and find in it life anew.
I invoke it in every breath, and seek what's True.

Prashna Upanishad (Atharvaveda)

When questions arise in my mind, Guru Pippalada whispers there.
Dwell in Atman & you'll find the answers to your prayer.

Mundaka Upanishad (Atharvaveda)

When I think of higher things, I reach an upper sphere.
Down below I don't sing, I'm a golden bird here.

Mandukya Upanishad (Atharvaveda)

"Who am I", I ask again & again, awake, asleep and in my dreams.
Why's reality so far from plain? Why isn't all as it seems?

Taittriya Upanishad (Yajurveda)

When I learn & I teach, I take & give back what I can.
All dark corners my light must reach, & that's what I plan.

Aitereya Upanishad (Rigveda)

I know all knowledge is divine, and I must learn from everyone.
Only then will this world be mine and I'll be ALL under the sun.

Chandogya Upanishad (Samveda)

Uddalika's words echo in my mind - All comes from naught & ends there.
In this 'nothingness' I'll find, what I seek everywhere.

Brihad Aranyaka Upanishad (Yajurveda)

Complete in myself, fully free,
I am all that I can be.

I am That all the time
I am its prose, I am its rhyme.

Not for me pilgrimages galore
Or visits to seers door.
Wherever I look, there I am
My holy land is where I am.

And so,
I sleep well and come the dawn,
I smile at another day,
To face again the devil's spawn
And all else, come what may.

Our own demons...

I couldn't kill my demons once for all,
For they're immortal as you know.
They enter you if you were to fall,
They strike when you're low.

They poison your heart & your mind,
And you become like them too.
Then one day you sadly find,
Your world has a demon new.

I threw the demons in my heart,
Where they couldn't easily follow.
I then took myself apart,
And remade me without the hollow.

If there's no place in you for these,
If you have no hollows in you,
They can do as they please,
But they can't enter you anew.

I caught mine well in time.
I ask you now to look inside.
They hide in places not sublime,
They hide where love has died.

So seek them in corners dark,
Catch them hissing in their lair,
Make your goodness light a spark,
And set them all afire.

Then if you find any again,
Or they find you, when you're low,
Think of the grief & the pain,
They caused you some time ago.

They hypnotize you with their sight,
But do not ever become their pawn.
Shun them with all your might,
Step on them and move on.

ᘓᘔᘓᘔᘓᘔ

Shiva & Shakti

I am convinced, somewhere between Shiva and Shakti, lies the secret of the universe

When I contemplate his magnificient roops - Bhutesh, Vamdevo, Mahadevo, Neelkantha, Viruupaakshas-trilochanaH, ShambhuriishaH, PashupatiH, ShivaH, Shuulii, MaheshvaraH

Lord of the ashta-siddhis, aNimaa, mahima, garimaa, laghimaa, praaptiH, praakaamyam, iishitvaM, vashitvaM; Escorted by Ekdanta, Lambodar, Vighnavinashak, Ganpati, ShikhivaahanaH, ShhaaNmaaturaH, ShaktidharaH, Kartikeya and myriad fearsome rakshasas, astride the divine Nandiko nandikeshvara;

I am filled with awe,

But then I see, beside him the divine mother, Shree personified,

Uma, Kaatyaayanii, Gaurii, Kaali, Haimavatiishvarii, Shivaa-bhavaanii, RudraaNii, SharvaaNii, SarvamaN'galaa, AparNaa, Paarvatii, Durgaa, Mr'iDaanii, ChaNDika, Ambikaa;

And I wonder,

As some say, will Shiva become 'shava' if Shakti moves away? Who, then, will I find in the silence between breaths?

Mother Night told me…

Last night, on my balcony, as I was silently watching the day end, I felt the night call my name…

Bats swooped around like manic flyers,
The night owl hooted its questioning cry,
Cicadas played their orchestra below,
The night was unhappy, I heard it sigh.

'The twilight was too short', it said,
'The day couldn't tell me more,
And at dawn, it'll have forgotten all,
Of that I am very sure.'

There were questions left unasked,
Many mysteries still unravelled.
My love had no time to feel fulfilled,
On the paths that we had travelled.

We weren't together in one place for long,
Yet I am the mother of the dawn,
And in me it dies, when the day is done,
As I die in it, every morn.

That's what mothers do, I am told,
They live and die again and again,
Long after they have forgotten,

Their unimaginable birthing pain.

The twilight ends for them too,
When their baby is no longer so,
Just like for me, it is too short,
So much love left yet to grow.

That's the cycle of life, I now realise,
You go, sleep now, let your dreams flow,
And if, perchance, you meet your mother,
Give her my love, tell her I know!

ꕥꕥꕥ

My Ego and ME

I am ancient, trying to keep my body, my vehicle for a short while, this time around, as fit as I can, as long as I need to use it here.

I am ancient, trying to keep my mind, my motor for a short while, this time around, as well-oiled as I can, as long as I keep learning.

My ego, masked as 'I', rides on the result, using the mind, to look at the body, preening and proud, full of glee, as if it has anything to take credit for.

What a poseur!

One day, I will remove its mask, and, naked, it will fade away, like a shadow in the light. Till then, I let the illusion be & the masked one pose as me.

This could cause confusion in the unwary, between the ancient and the new, the permanent and the temporary, the witness and the witnessed.

However, I know it well for what it is, an ephemeral pretender, wearing a prop, acting in a short play. I watch it, amused, often laughing at its pretensions.

But I learn from its mistakes so that these are not repeated in future plays. And so, I pass my days, waiting and watching, ere I move on to my egoless world, where masks aren't needed, where 'I' is just ME, and all is as it should be.

Time, yours and mine

As a potter moulds his clay into a thing of beauty, let's shape time as our fondest dreams, so that we are complete in each other and all around us shines our joy, making fulfilment more than a word and time more than a passage, for you and me, and all we touch.

ꟹ

Intimations of Mortality

Shelley's Liguria lives, in all its beauty, but he is no more and Byron or others like them. The romance is alive, well past the romantics and one day, we too will go away, leaving behind us, this blessed Earth and the hope, that we leave it such that it can shower its blessings, on those who may follow, as it has, on us.

ଔଷଔଷଔଷ

Depression, Hope and a Prayer

Depression

With scowling faces & lowered brow,
Ghosts the colour of eigengrau,*
Populate nightmares night & day,
Leaving you helpless in their grey.

No hope is felt, no colours bright,
The body, mind find nothing right,
Silent sobs, unheard, unseen,
No one knows where you've been.

Eyes closed all is dark,
Eyes open the world is stark,
Loneliness, deep, profound,
All around like surround sound.

When you're in this morass,
Inside your private cage of glass,
You often feel you'd better be dead,
Than alive in perpetual dread.
****

Hope….

If you're one of the fortunate few,
You'll come across someone new,
And with this sunrise in your sky,
You'll see your evil demons fly.

Someone gentle holding your hand,
Someone who can understand,
Your inner fears, your ghosts of yore,
Someone true, caring, pure.

When this happens, then you must,
Return their trust with your trust.
Open your heart, be fearless, free,
And if all goes well, you will see.

New hope of life in your world,
Well lit, your joy unfurled,
With someone close, your fears gone,
You'll find yourself reborn.
****

Prayer

That's my prayer to all god-kind
May everyone so afflicted find
An angel to lead them into the light
Where colours abound & all is bright

Amen….
****

* Eigengrau – the grey-black colour we see when we close our eyes in the dark.

My Mind & Me....

My mind's a useful tool, user of my brain,
Keeping me from being a fool, just this side of insane.

I often roam the roads, that dot the insides of my mind,
Among the wonders there aplenty, this I always find.

My mind dances and so it will, till the end of time,
The last dance will be goodbye, and it'll be sublime.

My mind and I will then part, with grateful thanks from me,
I'll take with me what it has taught, that's how it'll be.

Parting's not sorrow here, no sobs or cries or wails,
A book I've read cover to cover, just leaves me with its tales.

Another day will dawn anew, another brain another mind,
Carefully chosen by my Self, to learn what I left behind.

ᏡᏕᏅᏡᏕᏅᏡᏕᏅ

At Bedtime

I evoke all the 'me's that were here before 'I'. As I sleep, come whisper your wisdom in my mind so that I can be the best of who I have been.

I evoke all the 'me's that are yet to be, after I am no more. As I sleep, come and guide me so that when I leave, I carry what will be of most use for your fulfilment when you are 'I'.

And, finally, I evoke all the Masters who have guided me through aeons, birth after birth to bring me where I can 'feel' their love in my being. And, I pray you will continue to guide me till I am worthy of becoming one of you.

With these thoughts, I close my eyes and drift off into dreamland, hoping all of you are listening to me, who is now who you will be and who is now who you were once. And my Masters too, whose wisdom has and will always nurture all the 'me's and whose grace will continue to ennoble all of us.

Sharara

– the spark…

I don't want this or that, I want it all.
I want sun in the winter of my life, I want the spring in fall,
And when so many are walking bent, I want to stand tall.

Yes, I don't want this or that,
I want it all.
In quiet moments I hear me say, "No, I won't fade away."
There's a spark inside that doesn't die. It says, "go & try, you can fly."

"This is the time to learn new things. This is the time to decide,
Which poems will be written, which recipes tried."

"This is the time to plan for the future. This is the time to live.
This is the time to count my blessings. This is the time to give."

Am I too silly, am I a fool? No, I'm but old school.
We don't say die, till the end. We are real, we don't pretend.

I was born in another era, and I always hear its call –
Try your best and leave the rest, to fates' foot-fall!

Yes,

I don't want this or that,
I want it all.
I want sun in the winter of my life, I want the spring in fall
And when so many are walking bent, I want to stand tall.

Yes, I don't want this or that,
I want it all
And I well know
– it's up to me, to make it so....

Of Birth and Rebirth

This breath that comes and goes,
These nerves from head to toes;
This mind that's never still,
Always there to impose its will.

This heart beating day & night,
This face, often showing my plight.
These muscles, strong but fading fast,
These eyes & ears that won't last.

These cravings daily born anew,
These biases, most untrue.
This hair, here and gone tomorrow,
All these, I had to borrow,

To experience life in all its glory,
To learn through a new story
And when this story of mine is done,
I will craft another one.

One by one every time,
A rung on the ladder, I aim to climb.
Sometimes slipping sadly down,
When I believe I'm my gown.

This will happen again and again,
Till this ‘I’ doesn’t remain,
And everything that we can see,
Becomes me – just only me.

ଓଃଃଓଃଃଓଃଃ

My Mahabharata

Dhritrashtra, blind to many things, and
Gandhari who chose to be so.
Bhishma Pitamah with his difficult choices,
all much like the me I know.

Pandavs & Kauravs live on in my psyche, a
vague line 'tween good & sin.
I've to decide who dies in my Kurukshetra,
and who I let win.

Krishna's advice is also here, very wise and
very clear.
Nudging my conscience now & then, but
mostly unheeded, I fear.

That, in a nutshell is my war, my Mahabharat
day & night.
Who will I opt to stand for? When will I
choose to fight?

My war's not as simple as Arjun's in his time.
I've to rise above the mundane, into the
sublime.
I have these five senses, and their kin, my
yearnings all.
Pandavs & Kauravs alive, keeping me in their
thrall.

To win my own great war, this is the sum of
my fears.
I have to kill them all, say our ancient seers.

Only then will victory be mine, only then will
I be free.
Past both Kauravs & Pandavs, lies al
Firdaus's key.

ଔଷଧଔଷଧଔଷଧ

Perchance to dream of good things…

Some nights, eyes closed, I find, I am in a hall
in my mind.

In corners dim, shadows loom,
Doors marked, worry, fear, omens of gloom.
Their voices like Sirens of old,
Sing alluring songs, flattering, bold.
Ornate and loud they beguile,
And tempt me to stay there a while.

Their evil they well hide,
Waiting patiently inside.
If I am pulled in deep,
I know I'll never sleep.
I shudder & say no,
I have other places to go.

I go past labelled doors,
'Wins', 'Losses', 'Sundry Chores'.
Though they keep appealing to me,
Nothing useful here I see.

I move on leaving these behind,
Not stopping till I find,
Doors of 'love', 'hope', such things kind.

They welcome me in their embrace,
So serene, so full of grace,
My perfect resting place.

I enter & under their spell,
I fall asleep feeling well.

Perchance to dream of good things…

ঞ্জজ্ঞঞ্জজ্ঞঞ্জজ্ঞ

The Truth of Me, & of you, too…

Many masks I've worn, many roles played, but none of them last. Many names I've had, fleetingly, in eons past. But, truth be told, I have no name. From a blissful place, sans sin or shame, an incipient god I am, here for a while, playing this game.

I forget often, so engrossing's the world, a tapestry of emotions, but even when I remember, I still go through the motions. The universe dictates & I play my role, the best I can, some lives as a woman, some as a man.

And so it goes, with every death, back where I belong. New learning, then, in every birth, till my swan song. Then, past this cycle, incipient no more, I'll be with my fellow divine. Inside I know, I've always been theirs, and they've been mine.

But till then, here I am, with a mask on my face, hiding my grace, in this play, acting as 'Me'. Sometimes serious, but often laughing, at the folly I see.

Pilgrim's Progress - In the realm of the Spirit

Amidst the chaos, whispers arise,
How can I shed my disguise?
A yearning deep within the soul,
To find the truth that'll make me whole.

In search of my real home,
Eagerly seeking, I go roam,
Among bubbling brooks, rustling trees,
Icy mountains, whispering breeze.

I crave this truth, pure and deep,
When awake and when asleep;
With inner eyes, I strive to see,
The boundless vastness I can be.

I meet saints & mystic sages,
Who've tread this path through the ages;
Transcending creeds & dogmas old,
In their ornaments, I see the gold.

In their wisdom I strive to find,
What lies past my mundane mind,
In realms unseen, where they dwell,
Past the chaos, where all is well.

They urge me to travel within,
To find the yang, for my yin
To Be the Spirit, that I'M for sure,
Divine essence, blameless, pure.

Behind the veils of mortal sight,
I travel on this path, so bright
All the while, my heart's aflame
With a fire I cannot tame.

Beyond the veil of earthly bounds,
My spirit sings to celestial sounds;
In meditation's tranquil embrace,
I touch my own radiant grace.

In Anahata, nature's shrine,
Mystic threads of truth entwine;
I find my essence, deep & true
And glimpse the Sacred, known by few.

Immense serenity I do find,
In holy ground, past the mind.
Silence weaves its mystic spell,
Nothing's left to hear or tell.

A new world unfolds, serene, bright,
A tapestry of the purest light.
Realised spirit, a well-lit flame,
Nothing's going to be the same.

In these realms without & within,
I embrace my truth, see life begin;
In the rays of my grace,
In my home……my resting place!

A Swaying Pendulum, I am

When my heart, speaks to my mind, we are One;
When my mind, speaks to my heart, I'm undone;

Across the river, a flute beckons, a bridge to cross;
On my shore, there's more, though mostly dross;

Winter comes, it's getting cold
I see snowflakes, the string grows old,

Where will I be, when it breaks?

ઝઇઝઇઝઇ

Aham Brahmasmiti — Fana

- Beyond you & me, past yours & mine

Full of bliss, born of the Divine, in complete silence for a while, I am just Brahma's smile.

All is quiet, only bliss I find, in my heart, past my mind. No questions arise, no how or why, I am ALL, when fades the 'I'.

It's amazing when all I see, is no 'other', only me. The feeling passes, alas too soon; I await the evening, it's still noon.

The Old Man and I – one morning

I look in the mirror, an old man looks back,
I try to be gentle, cut him some slack.

He's come far, through thick & thin,
Some good deeds, many a sin.

The outer & inner, aren't quite the same,
The body's frail but the mind's game.

The mind keeps dancing around,
The body prefers to stay aground.

The old one smiles, "we've had fun,
But I'm sure we're not yet done!"

"Together you and I will cope,
Till we're alive, there's hope"

"We'll admire beauty, praise grace,
Play with kids, make a face."

"Verses will be written, stories told,
Laughter echo, raucous and bold."

"We'll touch dew, walk on grass,
Gather friends, raise a glass."

I smile then, all is well,
We're alive in every cell.

And on that note, I move away,
Happy at what he had to say!

☙❧☙❧☙❧

For my fellow sailors, my journey so far…

I started my voyage years back, where the ocean was dark and deep.
Many monsters tried to drown me, I've sent them to the deep.
There were storms off & on and still waters too,
But I've learnt aplenty, on this ocean blue.

I'd come with a map, but lost it on the way,
When my ego on the tiller, led me astray.
I made many wrong turns, but that's in the past,
Now my Guru's flag flies on my mast.

Having fended off krakens, having muted Siren's song,
Now I see land ahead, where I truly belong.
I'll sail my boat wisely, till I reach that welcome shore,
Where those I loved are waiting, for me by the door.

Other boats will follow, with those I hold dear,
Who still have knots left, on this ocean here.
Our boats are not the same, but we sail together, true,

And the home we return to, is the same for me and you.

Let's laugh together meanwhile, life's given us this boon,
Till we meet on our home-world, to sail again soon,
For there's still much to learn, that only here can we find,
In these very fragile boats, donning our body mind.

I'll journey with you next, on some voyages more,
Till I realise in my being & am very sure
That all is One, and the Trinity, isn't really Three
We are the Creator & the Creation
Not just You and Me!

ଔଔଔ

I am Sanatan...*

Full of love for all benign humans, regardless of their belief,
Full of affection for all creation, one with every flower & leaf,
I am Sanatan...

My rivers are sacred, my forests, too,
I see the eternal, in the deepest blue,
I am a Sanatan...

Full of compassion for the helpless & poor,
The eternal witness, never the doer,
I am a Sanatan...

With bhasm, on my heart, but living a normal life,
In blissful calm, eschewing any strife,
I am a Sanatan...

In deep silence, I often dwell,
In the Real, for a spell,
I am a Sanatan...

To do good, birth after birth, till I birth no more,
To return to my divinity, when on this earth no more,
I am a Sanatan...

Then, the path will end at the door,
And I'll not need these labels any more
But till then,
I'll remain Sanatan for sure.

☙❧☙❧☙❧

* Sanatan - used here to signify 'eternal'.

My Life…

When I view the slivers of my,
I'm grateful to the givers of my life.

My parents of course, in my heart I find,
Who gave me this body mind.

My brothers who were so part of me,
In past slivers I often see.

Many teachers too are alive here,
Who taught me to think and dare.

And my closest friend, my sweet wife,
Wise & caring, full of life.

My children, too, in slivers aglow,
My ice in heat, my warmth in snow.

My grandchildren in new slivers now,
Such beautiful life-givers now.
I forget not my closest friends,
Helping mend my frayed ends.

And above all, my gurus wise,
Who taught me to my surprise,
Who I am beyond this act,
Who I am for a fact.

All these and some more,
Are my very life for sure.
As they are, so am I,
From my birth, till I die.

When the hall is empty…

Sometimes, eyes closed, lying in bed, when sounds are not, nor lights, I banish all thoughts.

When their hall is empty, I hear my heart sing its sweet songs, sometimes of gratitude, for bringing me here, often full of laughter for where I am, full of hope for where I'll be, and, now and then, full of love and belonging.

The hall fills up with magical sparkles dancing to these songs, each a blessing, a reward, if you will, for ridding my mind of the mundane.

Slowly the music fades and all is still. Thoughts buried deep trouble me not, as I move from one dream to another, in blessed sleep.

ઌઌઌ

Words...

So many words in the world, spoken and unspoken. So much prose. Also, its stylish sister, poetry, aplenty. Some in search of closure, some for revenge, much for venting feelings grave. Some for power, some for pelf, some for ego, we think as our self.

So many songs in praise of God. So many recitals for the Divine, all seeking peace of one kind or another.

These are waves and eddies, in the clear ether of existence, flickering reflections, the kinetic hiding the potential under the surface.

Only in absolute silence, when the surface is calm, the Truth of us, the Haq we are, shimmers and, beyond ideas and concepts, beyond words, uttered & unuttered, we find bliss.

Of Nothing & Everything

Does the murmuring swallow in the rear, hear
the command to turn?
Does the tree on the path of lava feels it
deserves to burn?

Does the electron that pledged troth to a
proton leave it for another?
Does the tiny turtle hatched on the beach
yearn for its mother?

Does a salmon know that a bear's claw will
capture it as it flies?
Is a star happy that it will be the brightest
when it dies?

Are tigers only leopards, whose colours ran?
Are horses donkeys, who said, we can?

Does the hungry lion have compassion for its
kill?
Is fate merely play-dough in the hands of our
will?

Does the virus causing havoc ever wonder
why?
Are all my thoughts immortal or do some die?

Does the Universe care that it was born of nothing at all?
Is the Earth conscious or just a mindless circling ball?

Is the scorching summer sun, boasting of its power?
Is humanity just a transitory Babel's Tower?

Does the earthquake bother about us and our kind?
Such questions sometimes light the neurons of my mind.

ꕥꕥꕥ

Carpe Diem

Seize the day, for yesterdays are gone,
And tomorrows are yet to be.
Seize the day, for you are here,
Grasp the treasure you see.

Seize the day, seize the day,
Ere it vanishes in mists of yore.
Seize the day for once it goes,
It won't come back no more.

ઉଓઉଓઉଓ

Between Thoughts…

I try to dwell in the gaps between thoughts,
Where silence prevails and all's serene,
Beyond mundane life and its plots,
Where words are neither heard nor seen.

Sometimes there I sense my soul,
The magical Self that I can be,
But thoughts intrude past these gaps,
And I lose sight of the real me.

I know the truth but that's not enough,
Till I keep acting in this play,
Where ego tells me what to do,
And ego tells me what to say.

My mask I have firmly on,
My script is also always here,
But in these gaps between thoughts,
My soul & I are very near.

And will one day, become One...

My Way

My loved ones do hold me tight, and I revel in them at work and play, but I've been blessed with inner sight.

My glories here, and, often my plight, what people see, what people say, are not what I am, not quite.

War against shadows, many might, or give up, cry, kneel and pray, but that isn't really my fight.

And,

I rage not against the dying light, for I know that a brighter day, is there for me, after this night.

I go quietly, unbent, upright, calm & joyful on my way, without any anger, without any fright.

This Life & Then…

I found my smile,
When as a fresh leaf in spring,
I first felt dew,
And heard a bird sing.

I found joy,
When in the summer,
I gave shade to those in need;
When I loved my flower,
And tended our seed.

I'll find my divine,
When, after a full life,
In blessed fall,
From one, I'll be None
And then, All.

My Genesis and my Destination

I have discovered inside me, an ancient secret which has brought us where we are today. And, knowing the path which we have come by, I know the Tao back,

One day, in the mirror I saw the Tree of Knowledge mocking me, upside down, its roots my hair, the trunk my spine and the myriad branching webs of my nerves, the arbiters of my senses. And, just then, the stirring of Kundalini at the base of my spine, reminded me of the Serpent, coiled, tempting, at the core of this Tree, connecting it to the Divine. And I knew beyond doubt, my own Genesis and my destination.

In the beginning was dust From this "adamah" Adam was formed and his spirit included Eve. Indeed, originally, Adam was One, entirely whole, neither man nor woman, yet, spiritually complete and in harmony with all Creation, sharing many aspects of the Divine.

Then Hawwa appeared, Life, separate, yet wed to Adam and was named Eve. They ate the fruit from the Tree of Knowledge. Having lived with this Tree and tasted myself this fruit, I realized that this had to be. With life, Ego had arisen, and Desire, both enough to undo mankind. The Serpent was blamed unfairly, though, indeed, its stirrings could unsettle the unwary.

From this Fruit all was learnt. Tov wa-ra taught Good and Evil, Life and Death, Love and Hate, God and Satan, "You" and "Me", Mine and Thine, Man and Woman, Terefah and Kosher, Nude and Covered, and so, from One, many Twos came to be.

Though it is said, Eve was made from Adam's rib, it was behind it that arose the desire of his heart. If you doubt this, count the 24 ribs of your son and daughter. There are none that are missing in your son.

The Garden of Eden is no Garden forsooth as we know such things. It is a blessed continuum where only those can stay, who are One, in tune with it.

Being Two, Adam and Eve were banished from this heaven, but inside them a part of it remained and many centuries later, it passed on to me as my inheritance from the Divine. As also, an inheritance from my forebears, the taste of the fruit from the Tree of Knowledge, powerfully coloring all I sense.

From this life and past ones, I know within me, this Paridezia exists and, one day, I will forget the taste of the fruit and, shunning the

Tree of Knowledge, egoless, will return to Edinu where Adam and Eve were once One. I will then be entirely whole, neither man nor woman and yet, spiritually complete and in harmony with all Creation.

Then, I can declare that in truth I was always, them, and, if I am to believe Ben-Sira, Lilith, too. Older than Eve and Adam's equal, much maligned for refusing to submit. All hiding behind the dream created by the fruit of the Tree of Knowledge that even now resides in me and mediates all I sense.

ଔଓଔଓଔଓ

Satori: The Path Unfolds

Tonight, I will dream of you, my killers and weave the fantasy of your death in my life. When the veil of sleep lifts, the imagined and the real, may be one if my dream is vivid enough.

You are a thousand strong and I am but one, but you know me not and I know you alas, only too well. I have seen your face, I have noticed the blood on your hands, I have tasted the poison brewed by you. I have called your name and found it wanting in essence, in truth.

You do your work, day and night, with stealth and without, sounding drums, which deafen, beguiling all with myrrh and frankincense, offering bribes of milk and honey, birthing fear where none need be, plying your wine till all are blinded and in your thrall.

The world painted in your colours, the real hidden behind the magic of your craft, the One divided in many parts. Other 'I's here I should be.

I, too, have been busy. I have glimpsed the truth, amassed evidence and found a forum for your trial.

It is the Court of Silence

The Judge speaks not, the jury, too sits absorbed and me, I am a silent witness. Not a leaf stirs in the mind, no taste is there, of forbidden fruit, no thoughts – your agents, can intrude.

You may say the trial is unfair, for the judge, the jury and the witness are one but, who are you to cry foul? You, who know all the tricks and have practised these, without scruples for millennia.

In this court, you cannot speak or dance, or paint, and the empty canvas shines untainted. All your wiles have no say, all your spells go astray. Milk and honey lose their allure, tempting libations are no more, and fear, that coward, cowers by the door.

There is no defence you can advance, no ploy you can use, but your call has come and you can't refuse. Try my killers, as you wish to prolong your life the 'I' you spin on the 'I' I am, imprisons no more. The star witness is finally free. His feet are finally on the other shore.

And now,

Truth prevails, in this court. In its light all is clear as it was the day of my birth ere I became a slave on this earth. Your deeds exposed all barriers fall in the nothingness from whence they sprung & all the Plural fade away. That which was never alive cannot face the light of day.

Yes, I can see all, in fair detail - the long night nears its end. Shadows are no more, and I awaken to a new dawn.

WE ARE WHOLE!

All over the world we find,
That those who've stilled their mind,
Hear this in their hearts,
"We are whole, not just parts!"

ଓଃଓଃଓଃ

Brahmasmi: Upanishads
Shivoham: Adi Shankaracharya
Ma fi Jubbati illa-Allah: Mansour al Hallaj
The heart has eyes which the brain knows nothing of: Ram Dass
The game is not about becoming somebody; it's about becoming nobody.
Charles H. Perkhurst
I am That: Nisargadutta Maharaj
Know thy Self: Esho'a
Be as you Are: Ramana Maharshi
"Gnothi se auton":
Inscription on the Sun god Apollo's Oracle of Delphi temple in ancient Greece

ଓଃଓଃଓଃ

Contents

www.ingramcontent.com/pod-product-compliance
Lightning Source LLC
LaVergne TN
LVHW091258150826
845673LV00006B/1466

* 9 7 9 8 8 9 1 8 6 9 3 7 0 *